COOK BOOK
Gertrude Stein, William Cook
and Le Corbusier

ERRATA Cook's wife's family name is mistakenly spelled throughout. It should be MOALLIC not Maollic. Email address <sassoonorlater@gmail.com>

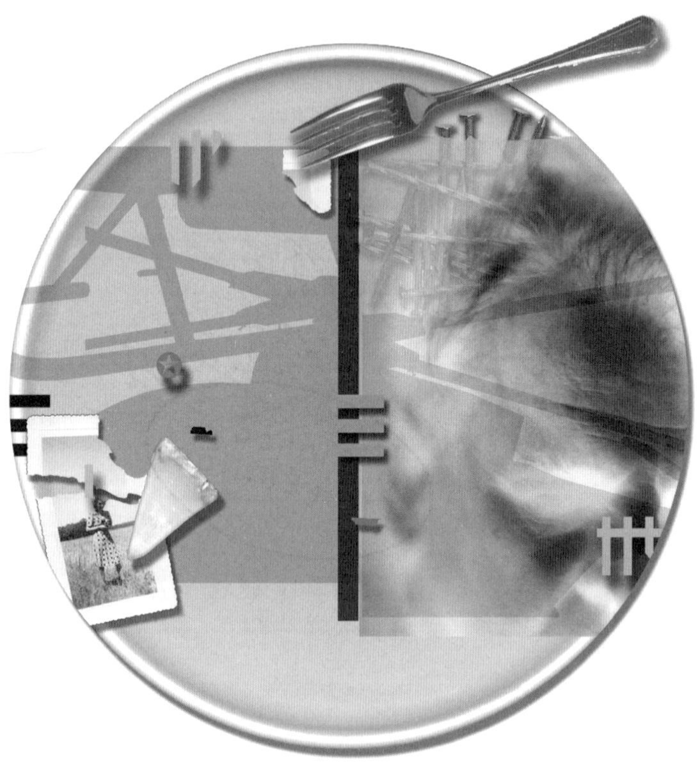

■ A cook does not mean that there is cooking.

—GERTRUDE STEIN
(1933b)

■ As if a cookbook had anything to do with writing.
—ALICE B. TOKLAS

Roy R. Behrens

COOK BOOK:

Gertrude Stein, William Cook and Le Corbusier

—with visual poems for Gertrude Stein

■ I was only four years old when I was first in Paris and talked French there, and ate soup for early breakfast and had leg of mutton and spinach for lunch, I always liked spinach, and a black cat jumped on my mother's back.

—GERTRUDE STEIN
(1940)

BOBOLINK BOOKS / 2005

THIS BOOK is dedicated to all those people who, like Gertrude Stein and William Cook, have had the courage to be expatriates (literally or metaphorically)—who have dared to swim against the tide of orthodoxy.

Cook Book:
Gertrude Stein, William Cook
and Le Corbusier

published by
Bobolink Books
2022 X Avenue
Dysart Iowa 52224-9767 USA
E-mail <ballast@netins.net>

Copyright © 2005 by Roy R. Behrens.
All rights reserved. First edition.
ISBN 0-9713244-1-7

With the exception of brief passages for the purpose of reviews, no part of this book may be reproduced in any form or by any means, electronic or mechanical, including photocopying, recording, or by any information storage and retrieval system, without the written permission of the publisher.

Printed in the United States of America

■ Before food was invented, books about cooking were unknown.

—FRED ALLEN

Frontispiece:
ROY R. BEHRENS *What Does Cook Want To Do?*
Visual Poems for Gertrude Stein, 2004.
Digital collage.

Menu

■ I would like to have seen Iowa. Carl [Van Vechten]
and [William] Cook come from Iowa, you are bril-
liant and subtle if you come from Iowa and really
strange and you live as you live and you are always
very well taken care of if you come from Iowa.

—GERTRUDE STEIN
(1973a)

■ [In *Star Trek*, Captain] Kirk is
eating pizza in a joint in San
Francisco with a woman whose
help he will need, when he
decides to fess up about who
he is and where he has come
from. The camera circles the
room, then homes in on Kirk
and his companion as she
bursts out with, "You mean
you're from outer space?" "No,"
says Kirk, "I'm from Iowa. I just
work in outer space."

—MARVIN BELL
A Marvin Bell Reader
(1994)

Introduction
With Comments by the Maitre d'

THE TITLE of this book is of course a *jeu de mots* or "play on words," since it is not really a cookbook but a Cook book—a book about a man named Cook. It is a biographical sketch of a largely unknown artist named William Edwards Cook.

Born in the last quarter of the 19th century in a small midwestern town, Cook left the U.S. in 1903 to study art in Europe, and thereafter continued to live overseas as an expat (or expatriate) as well as a minor participant in what Gertrude Stein called the "lost generation." Nearly all his adult life was spent in France, Italy and Spain—in Paris, Rome and Palma de Majorca, respectively. Only rarely and reluctantly did he return to the U.S. to visit, and, when he did, it was almost always briefly.

By coincidence, William Cook and I grew up in the same small town in Iowa. As a child, I too imagined that I might someday become an artist, and by age seventeen, like Cook, I too could not ignore the allure of more colorful settings.

Cook died in 1959, when I was in the eighth grade. But he was living in Spain then, and had not set foot in America for twenty years. I had not even heard his name, although (as I would later learn) some of his relatives were among my schoolmates, and indeed they owned some of his paintings.

Not only was I unacquainted with Cook in those days, most likely I also knew nothing about Stein and Le Corbusier. As this book documents, it was these two luminaries (and earlier, to a lesser extent, Pope Pius X) who made lasting contributions to Cook's legacy, in the sense that they provided the grounds for his own limited celebrity.

To follow, whenever Cook is remembered today, it is nearly always for two reasons: First, he was a close and loyal friend of Gertrude Stein and Alice B. Toklas, and in fact he was Stein's driving instructor when (wanting to contribute to the American Fund for French Wounded during World War I) she learned how to drive a car. Second, when his father died in 1924, Cook used part of his parents' inheritance to hire a then unknown young architect named Le Corbusier to design a starkly Modern house called Villa Cook or Maison Cook on the outskirts of Paris, in Boulogne-sur-Seine, a house that was contributive to that architect's development.

I first became curious about Cook about twenty years ago, while nosing around in Stein's memoirs, in which he is frequently mentioned. From there, the rest was sleuthing—and what you see here are the findings from that.

Near the end of this book, in a section called "gratuities," I have listed the people and agencies who have contributed to my work,

> ▨ Many excellent cooks are spoiled by going into the arts.
>
> —PAUL GAUGUIN

including Cook's relatives, prominent Stein scholars, various libraries and other institutions, my university colleagues and students, and residents of the Iowa town where he and I both originated. I am grateful to all of them.

As I continue to age, I realize increasingly that whatever I may have accomplished in the past twenty years of my life (as a writer, a teacher, an artist) has been made possible by the limitless love and devotion of my extraordinary wife, artist Mary Snyder Behrens. ■

—ROY R. BEHRENS
27 June 2004

■ I imagined asking her whether she liked Le Corbusier, and her replying, "Love some, with a little Benedictine if you've got it."

—PETER DE VRIES
Tunnel of Love
(1958)

■ Every human being on this earth is born with a tragedy, and it isn't original sin. He's born with the tragedy that he has to grow up. That he has to leave the nest, the security, and go out to do battle. He has to lose everything that is lovely and fight for a new loveliness of his own making, and it's a tragedy. A lot of people don't have the courage to do it.

—HELEN HAYES

We are all Americans at puberty; we die French.

—EVELYN WAUGH

One / Lentil Soup

When Good Americans Die
They Go To Paris

■ In short, my dear Sir, we take the world, and the things in it, as they are; it is a dirty world, but, like France, has a vast number of good things in it.

—PHILIP THICKNESSE
*A Year's Journey
Through France
and Spain*

■ Bouillabaisse is only good because cooked by the French, who, if they cared to try, could produce an excellent and nutritious substitute out of cigar stumps and empty matchboxes.

—NORMAN DOUGLAS
Siren Land
(1948)

■ The cook was a good cook, as cooks go; and as cooks go, she went.

—H.H. MUNRO
Reginald on Besetting Sins

■ I don't see why people make such a to-do about choosing a new cook. There is only one thing that is absolutely essential. I always ask at once, "Do you drink?," and if she says "No!," I bow politely and say that I am very sorry but I fear she will not suit. All *good* cooks drink.

—JAMES A.M. WHISTLER

■ The moon follows the sun like a French translation of a Russian poet.

—WALLACE STEVENS

■ There is no such thing as a Paris that everyone knows, that may be captured and put into a guidebook or a volume of whimsical reminiscences, for the benefit of the tourist or curiosity-seeker. It was always *somebody's Paris*. It always has been and always will be.

—SAMUEL PUTNAM
(1947)

■ At last! Someone who speaks French.

—COLETTE
[to a cat that meowed
at her on a New York
street]

—

Figure 1.A
ROY R. BEHRENS *The
Last Time I Saw Paris*
Visual Poems for
Gertrude Stein, 2004.
Digital collage.

■ What is so good is that you can be gentle to Iowa. Iowa is gentle.

—GERTRUDE STEIN
Letter to
Carl Van Vechten
(Burns 1986)

■ …if you see him [the writer Hart Crane] speak to him for me I am very fond of him he is so sweet he might almost come from Iowa…

—GERTRUDE STEIN
Letter to
Carl Van Vechten
(Burns 1986)

■ You, who have ever been to Paris, know; And you who have not been to Paris—go!

—JOHN RUSKIN
A Tour Through France

■ [When Sammy "the Bull" Gravano agreed to cooperate with the FBI in prosecuting John Gotti and other members of the Gambino crime family, an initial meeting was arranged between Gravano and a federal agent named Bruce Moaw. The meeting began in the following way:] Bruce Moaw walks over and shakes my hand [recalled Gravano]. He opened the door and I got in. I told him, "Are you Moaw?" He says, "Yes," and I said, "I heard you were from Iowa."

He said that was right and I said, "Well, if I got to trust somebody, it might as well be somebody from Iowa." And off we went.

—SAMMY
"THE BULL" GRAVANO
in Peter Maas, *Underboss*

■ It was so cold in Iowa this winter we saw a lawyer on the street with his hands in his own pockets.

—ANON

■ Iowa–corn-fed absoluteness—want to be one big family—to have a "crowd"—our "crowd" etc.—their "crowd."

—THOMAS WOLFE
Notebooks

■ I had forgotten how flat and empty it [the Midwest] is. Stand on two phone books almost anywhere in Iowa and you get a view.

—BILL BRYSON
The Lost Continent

■ I had always assumed that cliché was a suburb of Paris, until I discovered it to be a street in Oxford.

—PHILIP GUEDALLA

■ There's something Vichy about the French.

—IVOR NOVELLO

■ [Sardi's in New York is] where I had my first experience with cold potato soup, which is supposed to be a delicacy. I told my wife, I said, "If you ever brought me a bowl of cold potato soup out of the kitchen I'd turn around and ask you to heat it up! Vichyshwash or whatever. That's gotta be a big-city ploy if I ever heard one."

—DUANE WEST
New York Times Book Review
December 28, 1997

■ I'd found the answer [to how and what to paint] when I joined a school of painters in Paris after the war who called themselves neomeditationists… They believed an artist had to wait for inspiration, very quietly, and they did most of their waiting at the Café du Dome or the Rotonde with brandy. It was then that I realized that all the really good ideas I'd ever had came to me while I was milking a cow. So I went back to Iowa.

—GRANT WOOD
quoted in
Art and Antiques
(January 1989)

■ [Gertrude Stein] liked to take a chair and sit in a person's life.

—PAVEL TCHELITCHEV
Journal

■ [Iowa-born writer Carl Van Vechten] did not stay long enough really to qualify as a native son and, once he escaped, he never longed to rejoin the alien race from which he fled in 1899. Cedar Rapids [Iowa] was like one of its customary midday meals: wholesome and plentiful, unimaginatively but well cooked, on which one might grow. To stick around for second helpings, however, could only induce indigestion: the corn belt had a way of stealthily tightening around the belly.

So he was born in Iowa, and he got out just as soon as possible.

—BRUCE KELLNER
(1968)

■ I have a weakness for Iowa. Iowa is different
from the others.

—GERTRUDE STEIN
Letter to Carl Van Vechten
(March 17, 1924)

Two / Mirrored Eggs

America Is My Country
But Paris Is My Hometown

GERTRUDE STEIN and William Cook were quintessential "Americans in Paris." Both were expats (or expatriates) who moved, separately, in 1905 to Paris, the partly figmental metropolis known as the City of Lights.

In that year, Stein was 29 years old, while Cook was only 22. In their remaining lives, both would return to America to visit: Stein came back only once, for an extended book publicity tour, while Cook returned briefly a number of times. But neither moved back to the country they loved—if preferably from a distance—the place that they fondly referred to in conversation and correspondence as "our native land."

Stein, an avant-garde Modernist writer, patron of the arts, and art collector, was born in 1874 in Allegheny, Pennsylvania, a suburb of Pittsburgh, lived briefly in Europe, then moved to Oakland, California (about which she later said "there is no there there"[2.1]), where she spent the majority of her childhood. When she died in France on July 27, 1946, while undergoing surgery for cancer, she was buried in the historic Père-Lachaise cemetery in Paris, where her tombstone mistakenly claims she was born in "Allfghany" and that she died on July 29 (the

I have lived half my life in Paris, not the half that made me, but the half in which I made what I made.

—GERTRUDE STEIN

One can be an expatriate without leaving his native soil.

—SAMUEL PUTNAM
(1947)

———

Figure 2.A
ROY R. BEHRENS
How Yuh Gonna Keep Em Down on the Farm
Visual Poems for Gertrude Stein, 2004.
Digital collage.

■ For some years many of us considered Paris our Second Country, and I confess that whenever I had occasion to leave it and return to my First Country, my native land, the fear would come to me that I would never be so happy again.

—MATTHEW JOSEPHSON

(1962)

date of the death of her brother, Leo, one year later).[2.2]

Her close friend William Edwards Cook was an erstwhile society painter, who sometimes introduced himself as "an Ohio farmer,"[2.3] although he was never really a farmer, nor was he from Ohio. He was born in 1881 in the small Midwestern town of Independence, Iowa, and died in 1959 in his adopted home of Majorca, one of the Balearic Islands, just off the eastern coast of Spain. He and his devoted wife, a Breton-born artist's model named Jeanne Maollic, were buried in above-ground vaults in a suburb of the city of Palma de Majorca called Genova.

A half century after their deaths, few writers in history are as widely known or satirized as is Gertrude Stein (she was, said Clifton Fadiman, "the mama of Dada"[2.4]), while Cook is all but forgotten today. When the latter is remembered, it is rarely as an artist (in part because few of his paintings are extraordinary), but for his warm, unbroken bond with Stein and with Alice B. Toklas (Stein's lifelong companion), for having taught Stein to drive an automobile, and because he is mentioned admiringly in a number of her writings, in which she most often refers to him as Cook.

Almost never does she call him William Cook, nor Will, nor Bill—she just simply calls him Cook. "Cook does and he says and he is kind to all," she wrote of him in one of her books, "He understands all. He is so kind."[2.5]

In 1938, shortly after the publication of Stein's second volume of autobiography (titled *Everyone's Autobiography*), the American writer Robert McAlmon said one day to Cook that he had "been reading Gertrude's book over again, and she treats you better than anyone else. I

think she likes you." "I replied modestly," remembered Cook, "of course, she always did, and I always liked her."[2.6]

COOK'S HOMETOWN, which Gertrude Stein referred to as "the little Presbyterian community of Independence, Iowa,"[2.7] is the county seat of Buchanan County in the northeast section of the state. Today, it is a quiet town with a population of around 6,000. But in the early 1890s, when Cook was a teenager, it was one of most famous little communities in America. It had become well known as a horse racing center, a distinction that earned it the popular name of "the Lexington of the North."[2.8]

Figure 2.B
Charles W. Williams [shown here] brought short-lived international fame and fortune to Cook's hometown, when two stallions that Williams raised (named Axtel and Allerton) broke world trotting records. A few years later, when the U.S. economy crashed, Williams moved to Galesburg, Illinois, where he influenced another talented and idealistic young man, a poet named Carl Sandburg.

■ [C.W. Williams] was a medium-sized man with an interesting face. I thought his face looked like he had secrets about handling horses, yet past that there was a solemn look that bordered on the blank—I couldn't make it out.

—CARL SANDBURG
All the Young Strangers
(1953)

Independence became a horse racing center through the meteoric fortunes of Charles W. Williams, a telegraph operator and creamery owner from nearby Jesup, Iowa. Two mares that Williams purchased in 1885 gave birth in a single year to two famous stallions, named Axtel and

Figure 2.C
Shown here are two opposing views of Main Street in Independence, Iowa, made by Des Moines photographer F. J. BANDHOTZ with a panoramic camera in 1907.

Allerton, the very first colts that Williams had raised. Amazingly, both these stallions broke world trotting records, resulting in earnings substantial enough that Williams was able to publish a racing newspaper titled *The American Trotter*, build a combined magnificent opera house and three-story hotel called The Gedney,[2.9] and construct a unique kite-shaped race track on the west edge of Independence, on a section of land he referred to as Rush Park.[2.10]

The decline of Williams' fortune came in 1893, with a sudden collapse of the American economy. But not before he had raised several other extraordinary trotting horses, including a mare that he christened Maud S. That this little

Iowa town and its horses were nationally
known is confirmed by a passage from one of
Stein's books: "Cook used to tell us," she wrote,
that his hometown of Independence had
"turned into a wonderful place when the trotting races took place, and of course Maud S and

when I was little everybody knew the horse
Maud S came from there."[2.11]

COOK'S FATHER was Justin Cook, a prosper-
ous Iowa lawyer who owned ten farms in
Buchanan County and additional property in
California. His mother was Bessie (née Johnson)
Cook. There were seven children in the family,
but two died during childhood, and another
somewhat later.[2.12] Cook's older brother
Roy earned a law degree, then returned to
Independence to practice law. A younger
brother named Robert went to school at Yale
University, settled in New Haven, and became a
prominent orthopedic surgeon. Florence, his
younger sister, was a pianist who lived in New

■ The last time I saw
him [Williams] was on
a Q. passenger train
from Chicago to
Galesburg. He sat
quiet in a seat by him-
self. And I could no
more read his face
than I could twenty
years earlier.

—CARL SANDBURG
All the Young Strangers
(1953)

York nearly all her life, taught on occasion, traveled frequently, and never married.

Cook, Stein and Toklas loved to joke about Cook's Iowa upbringing and the not always pleasant relations among members of his family. In one of her letters to him, Stein recalls how Toklas and Cook had facetiously planned to syndicate the letters he exchanged with his parents, like droll episodes in a soap opera.[2.13] In one of Stein's brief (and especially puzzling) writings, titled "What Does Cook Want To Do," there is a cryptic account of the dynamics of Cook's family:

"His father believed in stitches. His mother in labor union. They did not discuss this. They said that plenty had been said. They had a daughter and three sons. They had a son. He was a man who went to bed on Sunday. Why did he wish to see himself. He did not wish to see himself. He saw himself shave. The other son was a young one. He was fighting. Not then. He was a victim. Not to a boat not to a cow, not to a chicken. He was not. He approved of everything."[2.14]

Cook's inclination toward art as a profession became apparent while he was still in high school. His ambitions were encouraged by Dr. Joseph McGrady, a free-thinking local physician who would later inspire another artist, Robert Tabor.[2.15] Cook remained grateful to "Doc McGrady" throughout his life, and, years later (by which time the aging physician was blind), he apparently made a great effort to visit him whenever he returned to his hometown.

Figures 2.D and 2.E
Photographs of undated oil portraits by WILLIAM COOK of his father, lawyer Justin Cook [above] and his mother, Bessie (Johnson) Cook [facing page]. Courtesy of Douglas and Ruth Hamilton.

As a student, Cook had developed an interest in the paintings of British artist J. W. M. Turner (made famous in the 19th century by the writings of British art critic John Ruskin), as well as those of the American expatriate artist John Singer Sargent, much of whose output consisted

of commissioned portraits of members of the upper class. (There are several sources that claim that Cook was even personally acquainted with Sargent.[2.16])

Like most professionals who had survived an economic crash, Cook's parents would surely have hoped that their son would become a doctor (as did his younger brother), a lawyer (like his father and older brother), or a businessman, so they must have been greatly distressed to be told that he wanted to become a professional artist.

Nevertheless, shortly after his completion of high school, he set off on a lifelong adventure by enrolling as a student at the Art Institute of Chicago.[2.17]

In the several years that followed, while he studied art in Chicago, it seems that Cook became allied with the social elite of that city, an

■ [Putnam's own expatriation began in] the prairies, that endless waving sea of green in summer, in other seasons an expanse of brown stubble or of snow. But flat, always flat! Anyone who has not been born and reared in the heart of the prairies will never be able to appreciate how intensely a boy can long for the sight of a mountain or for a glimpse of lake, sea, or river, something more than the dirty little half-dried-up creek that ran through the scant woods on the outskirts of the central Illinois village where I was born and where I lived until my late teens.

—SAMUEL PUTNAM
(1947)

Figure 2.F
WILLIAM COOK
Self-Portrait, no date.
Oil painting. Collection
of Jane Parish Yang.

■ Cook was a very
nice American. The
French liked him.

—CICELY GITTES
(1998)

achievement that may have been aided by the social and political prominence of his own family. (Today, on permanent display at the Hoyt Sherman Place in Des Moines, Iowa—site of the Des Moines Women's Club, but originally the mansion of the businessman brother of General William T. Sherman—is a portrait by Cook of one of Iowa's most influential businessmen and politicians.[2.18]) Through that, or in addition, Cook may have established ties with Chicago socialites through his own artistic efforts (in the manner of John Singer Sargent) by painting portraits of the rich.

What is certain (from Stein's writings) is that, about a decade later, by which time Stein and Cook were both firmly settled in Paris, he would typically bring along to the Saturday evening soirées at her apartment at 27 rue de Fleurus "a great many [people] from Chicago, very wealthy stout ladies and equally wealthy tall good-looking thin ones."[2.19]

Cook completed his training at the Art Institute of Chicago in 1902. He then moved to New York, where he lived at 380 West 22nd Street and studied for an additional year at the National Academy of Design.[2.20] As was then expected of aspiring young artists, his next destination was Paris, which was of course considered to be the undisputed art capital of the world.

AFTER ARRIVING in Paris in 1903, Cook studied at the Academie Julian with one of the most admired academic painters of the 19th century,

Adolphe-William Bouguereau, who was nearly 80 years old. As is well known, this was an especially volatile time for European and American art, since Modern Art was in rapid ascendancy, the French Academy in decline.

The antagonism between Modernism and the

French Academy is foretold in a wonderful story about Pierre Auguste Renoir, who, like Bouguereau, painted nudes, but in a loose Impressionist style (which Bouguereau had derided). While being fitted for glasses to correct his diminishing eyesight, Renoir brushed them aside and exclaimed, "Good God, I'll see like Bouguereau now !"[2.21]

In time, Cook would himself become a restrained Modernist whose artistic hero was Paul Cézanne. At the same time, for the rest of his life, he refused to join in with those Modernists who despised Bouguereau. Years later, he was still telling the story of how he would watch the old French master pick up a pencil and, with no hesitation and without even raising his hand from the page, he would create

Figure 2.G
In 1893, Chicago was the site of the World's Columbian Exposition (which Cook attended), earning it the nickname of the "Paris of the Prairies." A few years later, the real Paris (as seen in the above street scene, with the Paris Opera on the left) was itself reinvigorated in 1900 when it hosted a huge turn-of-the-century world's fair.

■ [In 1934, when an American businessman named Hickey and his wife visited Europe, being Catholics, they] sought an audience with the Pope. Mrs. Hickey approached His Holiness [Pope Pius XI] with great reverence, and was almost shocked out of her wits by what the Pope said. Speaking in English, he began: "I am glad to welcome you both to Rome, first because we are all children of the same Holy Mother, but also because I understand, Mr. Hickey, that you are the General Manager of the Gillette Razor Company, and, you know, I have used a Gillette razor for many, many years and I think it is a wonderful invention. But tell me, what *is* the matter with the blades?"

—H.L. Mencken
Diary (1989)

the most graceful and effortless drawings. Said Cook, "We should always admire the academic masters!"**2.22**

During this same time period, also at the Academie Julian, Cook studied with another widely recognized artist, Jean-Paul Laurens, who was known for his "history paintings," and whose reputation as a teacher was that of an uncompromising disciplinarian.

COOK'S AMBITION to make his living as a portrait painter received a sudden, significant boost in 1907 when his request to paint a portrait of Pope Pius X was approved while he was visiting Rome. This was presumably unexpected, in the sense that Cook was still quite young, inexperienced and unknown. In addition, his religious upbringing had been Protestant, not Roman Catholic. That he should be selected as the first American to paint Pope Pius X (who had been appointed only four years earlier) suggests the possibility of some behind-the-scenes maneuvering at the Vatican. Perhaps Cook's choice was helped along by one of the most powerful Catholics in America—James E. Quigley, the Archbishop of Chicago—who was an important advisor to the Vatican, and who played an active role in Chicago politics.

Whatever did or did not happen behind the scenes, we know that Cook's appointment was revealed to him unexpectedly one January day, while he was patiently waiting around at the Vatican. "To his [Cook's] great surprise and pleasure," reported a feature article in the

Chicago Daily News, "the Pope, smiling cheerfully, said yes, then hesitated, and the young painter expected him to mention some future time and his heart fell, but instead the words came, 'We can begin at once, if you are ready.' The first sitting took place immediately."[2.23]

From that moment on, it took nearly five months to complete the pontiff's portrait. Throughout all those months, Cook, who was required to wear a formal tuxedo during all sittings, "was in constant attendance at the Vatican, waiting for the Pope to call him to his library and grant him a short sitting during the rare intervals of his busy time. Sometimes it was between one audience and another, very often late in the day and when the lights were already lit in the papal apartments. The Pope seldom forgot his young friend, 'the painter,' as he loved to call him. In some cases when Mr. Cook had been waiting for several hours in the antechamber, refusing to believe the repeated communications of the members of the Pope's court, that His Holiness was very busy and all his time was taken up, a chamberlain would come to him direct from the Pope saying that a sitting of five minutes would be granted. The Pope, always cheerful, would pose and Mr. Cook, very careful not to lose a single instant, would commence his work, and very often the five minutes were stretched to half an hour."[2.24]

The finished portrait of the Pope (of which only a news photograph survives, because the painting itself was destroyed in a fire) prompted other dignitaries, religious and otherwise, to

■ When I was a child my mother said to me, "If you become a soldier you'll be a general. If you become a monk you'll end up as the pope." Instead I became a painter and wound up as Picasso.

—PABLO PICASSO

Figure 2.H
The reign of Pope Pius X ended in its eleventh year in 1914, when he died unexpectedly. Shown here is a news photograph of WILLIAM COOK's oil painting, *Portrait of His Holiness, Pius X* (1907). Courtesy of Douglas and Ruth Hamilton.

■ That month we went to Picasso's studio in Arles, which was then called Rouen or Zurich, until the French renamed it in 1589 under Louis the Vague. (Louis was a sixteenth-century bastard king who was just mean to everybody.)

—WOODY ALLEN
Getting Even
(1978)

Figure 2.1
Among the most famous Parisian artistic events during this period was a banquet in 1908 in honor of the French "primitive" Henri Rousseau. As interpreted in this preparatory pencil sketch by Iowa artist GARY KELLEY (1988), it was a memorable drunken affair at which Rousseau played the violin, a fight was staged, and a tipsy Marie Laurencin collapsed into the pastries. Among the guests that evening were Gertrude and Leo Stein and Alice B. Toklas. Notice the African mask.

commission Cook to paint their portraits as well.

Perhaps it was only coincidence that the person with the highest priority in all this was none other than Archbishop Quigley, who had been visiting the Vatican but by then had returned to Chicago. As a result, it became necessary for Cook to travel back to Chicago from Rome, complete a portrait of Archbishop Quigley, and then travel back again to the Vatican to begin comparable portraits of a handful of other religious dignitaries, apparently including Cardinal Francesco Satolli and Archbishop Robert J. Seton.

Meanwhile, Cook's alma mater, the Art Institute of Chicago—delighted by the stardom of one of its recent graduates—set aside a special room for a display of six of his paintings, while comparable debuts were also arranged in London and Paris.

Undoubtedly, Cook was initially pleased by this flow of opportunity, and perhaps he was even euphoric. But it cannot have taken long to realize that living in the spotlight of high society would allow him precious little time or opportunity to investigate other possibilities. If he were to ride on this wave of success and thereby confine his activities to formal portraiture, he would very soon be typecast as a dependably academic "society painter," in which case he would be despised by his more adventuresome Modernist friends. Whatever potential he had as an innovator, he now seemed destined to be known as a mere journeyman.

IN PARIS in the very year that Cook began his lackluster portrait of Pope Pius X, a Spanish artist named Pablo Ruiz Picasso (who was by coincidence the same age as Cook) created a scandalous ground-breaking painting of five nude prostitutes, the title of which, *Les Demoiselles d'Avignon*, was said at the time to refer, not to the city of Avignon, France, but to a brothel on d'Avinyó Street in Barcelona, Spain.[2.25]

The poses of the women in this painting are intentional allusions to cheesecake pornography, while they also satirize the poses of the figures in supposedly innocent classical scenes by

J.A.D. Ingres, Bouguereau and other Academic masters.

The painting was also disturbing because (in apparent disregard for stylistic consistency) the faces of these prostitutes are clearly based on tribal masks from Africa, which Picasso had recently learned about from an ad hoc collection of "primitive art" at the Ethnographic Museum at the Trocadero in Paris.

■ It takes a lot of time to be a genius, you have to sit around so much doing nothing, really doing nothing.

—GERTRUDE STEIN
(1973a)

Les Demoiselles d'Avignon was shocking not only to the uninitiated. When it was first seen by Georges Braque, the artist's close friend and co-worker, he said to Picasso: "It's as if you wanted to feed us scraps and give us gasoline to drink to make us spit fire!"[2.26]

But in time it would prove of importance, so important that, according to art historian John Richardson (whose statement is consistent with those of many historians), it was "the first unequivocally twentieth-century masterpiece, a principal detonator of the modern movement, the cornerstone of twentieth-century art."[2.27]

At the time, it is unlikely that Cook and Picasso were acquainted. But Cook was far from isolated, and despite his initial intention to be a competent portrait painter, he was also peripherally influenced by many of the forerunners of Modernism, including Henri de Toulouse Lautrec, Edgar Degas, Pierre Bonnard, Edouard Vuillard, and—as mentioned earlier—Cézanne, the artist he sometimes referred to as "the Messiah of modern painting."[2.28]

For the rest of his life, as his Majorcan friend Cristobal Serra recalled, Cook remained firmly convinced that he "would never see more light than he had seen in the East. The genius of Cézanne had delivered him forever from 'the darkness of Egypt.'" Whenever Cézanne's name came up in conversation, Serra continued, "to persuade Cook to change his opinion [about the preeminence of Cézanne] was about as likely as getting a Gothic cathedral to dance to a popular tune."[2.29]

■ Back home everyone said I didn't have any talent. They might be saying the same thing over here but it sounds better in French.

GENE KELLY
(as Jerry Mulligan)
American in Paris (1951)

■ Juan Gris, the Spanish cubist, had convinced Alice Toklas to pose for a still life and, with his typical abstract conception of objects, began to break her face and body down to its basic geometrical forms until the police came and pulled him off.

—WOODY ALLEN
Getting Even
(1978)

Picasso and Gertrude Stein had first met two years earlier, in 1905, shortly after she and her brother Leo had purchased one of his paintings. But no one seems to know for sure when or how Stein and Cook were introduced.

What does seem likely is that Alice B. Toklas

first encountered William Cook at the famous Paris apartment of Gertrude and Leo Stein, at 27 rue de Fleurus, on September 28, 1907, the Saturday just prior to one of the most important events in the Paris art world, the fifth annual exhibition of the *Salon d'Automne*, which was slated to open the following week.[2.30]

Toklas had only recently arrived in Paris from California, and was attending her first Saturday evening salon at the Stein apartment. Among the other guests that night (some of whom were invited to dinner, while others dropped by later) were Pablo Picasso and his mistress Fernande Olivier, Georges Braque, Guillaume Appollinaire, Marie Laurencin, Patrick Henry Bruce (descended from the orator Patrick

Figure 2.J
Modern-era art, design, and architecture were all to some extent opposed to the prescriptive practices that had been inherited from the Renaissance. Instead, they promoted a rosier view of the Middle Ages, the age that was responsible for the great Gothic cathedrals. On the Left Bank of the Seine, not far from Gertrude Stein's apartment at 27 rue de Fleurus, was one of the best-known examples of that, the Cathedral of Notre-Dame (built between 1160 and 1360).

◼ [At Henri Matisse's studio school in Paris] A hungarian was found eating the bread for rubbing out crayon drawings that the various students left on their painting boards and this evidence of extreme poverty and lack of hygiene had an awful effect on the sensibilities of the americans.

GERTRUDE STEIN
(1933a)

◼ Curie
of the laboratory
of vocabulary
she crushed
the tonnage
of consciousness
congealed to phrases
to extract
a radium of the word.

—MINA LOY
a poem about
Gertrude Stein
(Carpenter 1988)

Henry), Ethel Mars, Maud Hunt Squire, Henri-Pierre Roche, Ramon Pichot, Alfred Maurer, Hans Purrman—and William Cook. Also present was a young Russian artist named Olga Markusovna Merson, who later became a student of Henri Matisse (who painted a wonderful portrait of her in 1911) and who, according to Toklas, became "good friends" with Cook as well.[2.31]

In all her nervousness, Toklas mistakenly assumed that Braque was an American, but "a real American," she recalled later, "was William Cook, who had painted the portraits of the English duchesses and later of the Roman world, including a number of cardinals, but had given this up and betaken himself to etching."[2.32] It is possible that this was Cook's first appearance as well at a Stein soirée.

By 1910, Gertrude Stein's formerly close relationship with her brother Leo was rapidly disintegrating. Increasingly critical of her experimental writing, he was also voicing frequent doubts about her enthusiasm for Picasso's paintings. For several years, Toklas, who had been sharing a nearby apartment with a friend, had been spending nearly every day at the Stein apartment, typing letters and manuscripts, cooking meals on the maid's day off, and becoming increasingly intimate in her relationship with Gertrude Stein. In 1910, Toklas moved into 27 rue de Fleurus, for which Leo gave up his small study for her to use as a bedroom.[2.33]

Meanwhile, Leo fell in love with an artist's model (whom he eventually married), while the

rift with his sister continued. Finally, in 1913,
Gertrude and Leo decided to split. They divided
up their famous art collection (he took all the
Renoirs and a painting of apples by Cézanne,
while she held on to all the Picassos); she kept
the apartment in Paris, while he moved on to
Italy.

In their remaining years, Gertrude and Leo
spoke only once, and even that occurred
inadvertently when, caught off guard, they unexpectedly crossed paths on a street corner, and,
for a very brief moment, forgot to ignore one
another. ■

■ [Arriving uninvited at a Stein soirée, he was talking
loudly about Jane Austen and sex when Gertrude Stein
approached:] "Do I know you?" she said. "No. I suppose
you are just one of those silly young men who admire
Jane Austen."

…I was faced by Miss Stein, the tweedy man and Miss
Toklas. Already uncomfortable at being an uninvited
guest, I found the calculated insolence of her tone intol-
erable and lost my temper.

"Yes, I am," I said. "And I suppose you are just one of
those silly old women who don't."

The fat Buddha-like face did not move. Miss Stein
merely turned, like a gun revolving on its turret, and
moved imperturbably away.

The tweedy man did not follow her. Leaning towards
me, his moustache bristling, he said quietly, "If you don't
leave here this moment, I will take great pleasure in
throwing you out, bodily."

—JOHN GLASSCO
(1970)

■ I love Spain and things Spanish and Picasso!

—ALICE B. TOKLAS
Letter to Louise Taylor
(August 16, 1951)

Three / Cold Ham
with Lettuce Salad

The Man Who Taught
Gertrude Stein To Drive

NO DOUBT Gertrude Stein and Alice B. Toklas (who had clandestinely married in a "same-sex" understanding in 1908) were hoping to recover from Stein's painful dispute with her brother when, in 1913, they decided that they would vacation in Spain.

By chance, as they were looking at a map, they discovered the Balearic Islands, off the eastern coast of Spain. When they were on the ferry going from the Spanish mainland to the island of Majorca (where Frederic Chopin and George Sand had wintered together romantically in 1838-39), they were surprised and pleased to find among the other passengers their friend William Cook and his French female companion named Jeanne Maollic (whom he would eventually marry), an artist's model and *femme de ménage* (or housekeeper), who had been born in Brittany. By fortunate coincidence, Cook and Jeanne had also found Majorca on the map, and they too were visiting for the first time.[3.1]

As it turned out, the two couples greatly enjoyed each other's company, although it was too often at Jeanne's expense because she was the only one who spoke little or no English. They loved the delightful language mistakes

■ A rhomboidal woman dressed in a floor-length gown apparently made of some kind of burlap, she [Gertrude Stein] gave the impression of absolute irrefragability; her ankles, almost concealed by the hieratic folds of her dress, were like the pillars of a temple: it was impossible to conceive of her lying down.

—JOHN GLASSCO
(1970)

—

Figure 3.A
ROY R. BEHRENS
Irrefragability Paired
Visual Poems for
Gertrude Stein, 2004.
Digital collage.

that came from her valiant attempts to fit in. For example, in conversation with Cook, she referred to Toklas and Stein as "Mlle Tosca and Miss Steins," which, as Cook then explained in a letter to them, she justified as "good enough as I know who she means, and you are both so charming that you are not the people to make the 'chichi' over a little matter of names."[3.2]

During that first shared visit to Majorca, Stein and Toklas remained for only a few days, while Cook and Jeanne stayed on for months. Pretending to be a married couple in a strict and conservative Catholic society, they rented a chapel to live in.

Cook painted a portrait of their landlord "in my best American fashion," and, for the local curé, he created a particularly graphic painting of the martyrdom of St. Sebastian, which he sardonically described in a letter to Stein as "all peppered with arrows like a pin cushion, blood all over the place, beats a bullfight, and to add a small note of sentiment have friend Sebastian tied fast to the pine tree in front of the chapel, with the Cathedral in the background, if that doesn't send emotions up and down his [the curé's] backbone then I shall have to try to touch him in some less poetic manner."[3.3]

Majorca is one of the Balearic Islands, in the Mediterranean Sea, about 160 miles off the eastern coast of Spain

Figure 3.B
Composer Frederick Chopin and writer George Sand spent a romantic winter in the town of Vaddemossa on Majorca in 1838-39. Stein, Toklas and the Cooks, whenever they visited Majorca, always lived near Palma, the island's largest city. Specifically, they preferred to live in Terreno, a colorful hilltop suburb on the city's west edge. They traveled to bullfights in Inca. Robert Graves, Robert Creeley, and other writers and artists, eventually settled at Deyá, about 20 miles from Palma.

During this same vacation period, Cook also convinced Jeanne that she should try her hand at painting. In a letter to Stein and Toklas, he reported that Jeanne "finds painting so easy that housekeeping is really more fun, that it occupies your attention so much more and painting may be all right for a man who has nothing else to do and it's nice and easy a way to earn a living as any, but for real diversion there's nothing like housekeeping. If you have casseroles enough, you never know how anything is going to turn out and you always have to hurry to get things done and so you don't have time to worry about anything. On the contrary if you are painting, you only have to sit down and you commence to worry about everything."[3.4]

WHEN WORLD War I broke out in Western Europe in August 1914, Cook was touring Italy with members of his Iowa family, who were visiting Europe for the first time. Jeanne did not join them on that tour, perhaps because Cook and she had agreed that it was not an opportune time to introduce her to his parents, since the unmarried couple was "living in sin."

Surely, his parents would not have been pleased that Jeanne was a lowly "service worker" (a cleaning woman) and—far worse—that she had also been an artist's model, a woman who took off her clothing and posed in the presence of a group of men. (A few years earlier, as recalled by a later friend, Jeanne had

■ Not so dots large dressed dots, big sizes, less laced, less laced diamonds, diamonds white, diamonds bright, diamonds in the in the light, diamonds light diamonds door diamonds hanging to be four, two four, all before, go go go go go go, go. Go go. Not guessed. Go go.

—GERTRUDE STEIN
[imitating flamenco dance rhythms] in "Preciosilla"
(Stein 1962)

■ Do be careful of eating garlic particularly on an island.

—GERTRUDE STEIN
(1955)

posed nude for the figure of a muse in a mural on the ceiling of a Paris theatre, so that "if you wanted to look at her, how she had been several years before, you could go to the theatre and she was on the ceiling along with the other muses. They were all pretty plump…")[3.5]

■ There are two things in Spain which are not found elsewhere—flowers, lovely flowers in such abundance, and bullfights. I love both.

—CAROLINE OTERO

As for the war itself, Stein recalled, Cook's father "refused to believe it and explained that he could understand a family fighting among themselves, in short a civil war, but not a serious war with ones neighbors."[3.6] Because of the fighting, the Cook family tour ended abruptly in Naples. As he departed, Cook's father said to him "that he didn't blame me for not wanting to go back to America and said I never need to go if I didn't want to but my Mother had set her heart on my coming home for Christmas…and he guessed I'd better."[3.7]

As it turned out, Cook did not go home for Christmas that year. Instead, he and Jeanne spent Christmas Eve together in Barcelona. But before leaving Paris for Spain, he worked briefly (perhaps in association with the Red Cross) in an American infirmary where wounded French soldiers had been hospitalized.

Soon after, Cook and Jeanne settled in Palma de Majorca, where they were joined in April

1915 by Stein and Toklas, who would remain on the island for over a year. When the latter couple arrived, Stein remembered, "Cook met us and arranged everything for us William Cook could always be depended upon."[3.8] They lived at first along the bay, west of the heart of the city, overlooking the Cathedral of La Seu.

The two couples took long walks through the olive groves in the district of Genova (where Cook and Jeanne would later be buried), and also traveled inland to Inca to attend a bullfight, where Jeanne witnessed for the first time that gruesome ceremonial rite. As a housekeeper, she was an experienced food preparer, but she also had great empathy

Figures 3.C and 3.D
These vintage photographs (c1920) are scenes of the harbor at Palma de Majorca and its imposing Cathedral of La Seu.

■ I think that cars today are the exact equivalent of the great Gothic cathedrals.

—ROLAND BARTHES

for animals. As a result, she seems to have been wholly unappreciative of the supposed romance of the slaughter. Both Cook and Stein found it fascinating, but, according to Toklas, Jeanne "could only think of the worth on the market of an animal of that size." As the two

■ We went to the bullfights. At first they upset me and Gertrude Stein used to tell me [Toklas], now look, now don't look, until finally I was able to look all the time.

—GERTRUDE STEIN
(1933a)

Figure 3.E
Vintage photograph of a bullfight in Valencia, Spain (c1920).

■ I always remember Picasso saying disgustedly apropos of some Germans who said they liked bullfights, they would, he said angrily, they like bloodshed. To a Spaniard it is not bloodshed, it is ritual.

—GERTRUDE STEIN
(1933a)

couples left Inca that day, Stein remembered, "Jeanne said, looking out of the window of the train as the evening commenced, This is the hour when the poet works."**3.9**

Cicely Gittes, a British-born musician who would later become a close friend of the Cooks, confirmed that Jeanne "had a wonderful way with animals." She described in particular an incident in the 1930s, when she and her husband (the American painter Archie Gittes) accompanied the Cooks to a bullfight. Cook and Jeanne were seated near the front wall of the arena when a young bull jumped up suddenly and landed with its head on Jeanne's lap, where it drooled and slobbered on her skirt.

Everyone else in the audience was terrified and immediately scrambled for safety. But not Jeanne—instead, she simply leaned forward and, stroking the head of the traumatized creature, said repeatedly "Poor *bulle petite*. Poor *bulle petite*."**3.10**

OVER THE years, Gertrude Stein and her brother Leo had judiciously collected art, including Japanese *ukiyo-e* woodblock prints, and a variety of paintings by Paul Gauguin, Henri de Toulouse-Lautrec, Honoré Daumier, Eugene Delacroix, El Greco, Auguste Renoir, Vincent Van Gogh, Paul Cézanne, Maurice Denis, Pablo Picasso, Henri Matisse, Georges Rouault, Juan Gris, André Derain, Robert Delaunay, and others. As is evident from photographs of the interior of the Stein apartment, these and other works were hung in a tightly stacked arrangement (called "salon style") that virtually extended from floor to ceiling.

However enduring Stein's friendship with Cook, there seems to be no mention of her having purchased any of his paintings, nor did he apparently present her with one (although he did send paintings as gifts to his Iowa friends and relatives, if not always his finest works). Judging from their written correspondence, only rarely were artistic matters the subject of their conversations. Instead, they much preferred to talk about bullfighting, religion, their American upbringings, money, and a relatively new invention, the automobile. In a letter that Cook wrote to Stein in 1924, he tells her he

■ People think that bullfights in my pictures were copied from life, but they are mistaken. I used to paint them before I'd seen the bullfight so as to make money to buy my ticket.

—PABLO PICASSO
(Sabartés 1949)

■ This summer I saw Picasso after a bullfight in Arles, accosted with the gifts of live infants. With a stroke of charcoal he designs on a baby's naked ass, and returns this art to the parents. What will they do, skin the child? Refuse it a bath for decades?

—NED ROREM
(1966)

can hardly wait for a visit by her and Toklas, because they will then "have a couple of days to talk over spark plugs and amortissors and things that interest us and it will be nice."[3.11]

In 1915 (when the two couples were still living on Majorca), both Cook and Stein became concerned by the continuance of World War I (which pundits had predicted would soon be over). In the end, they decided that they should return to Paris to contribute in an active way to the French war effort.

Meanwhile, even though neither Cook nor Stein had ever driven an automobile, they had both become obsessed with the idea of owning one. When Cook and Jeanne moved back to France (in advance of Stein and Toklas) in December 1915, he found work in an automotive factory and also signed up for driving lessons ("I go every morning at seven o'clock to an *école de chauffers*," he wrote[3.12]). Soon after, he became employed as a Paris taxi driver, in the course of which he also test drove Renaults, new and otherwise, since the regular taxis had been confiscated by the French Army as a means of transporting soldiers to the front line. All this was perfectly suited to Cook, because he dearly loved to speed. Stein recalls in her first autobiography "how exciting it was when he [Cook] described how the wind blew out his cheeks when he made eighty kilometers an hour."[3.13]

When Stein and Toklas did return to Paris in 1916, it was Cook who gave Stein driving lessons in the middle of the hot summer days,

I don't object to foreigners speaking a foreign language; I just wish they'd all speak the same foreign language.

—BILLY WILDER
Avanti

"Ill fo manger, you know," says Mr Jobling, pronouncing that word as if he meant a necessary fixture in an English stable. "Ill fo manger. That's the French saying, and mangering is as necessary to me as it is to a Frenchman. Or more so."

—CHARLES DICKENS
Bleak House

using his two-cylinder Renault taxi cab. The long-range goal of all this was to enable Stein and Toklas, working as a team, to contribute to the French war effort by using her convert- ed Ford van named "Auntie" (which she had purchased through relatives in the U.S.) as a supply truck for the American Fund for French Wounded. Their van was named in honor of Stein's Aunt Pauline, "who always behaved admirably in emergencies and behaved fairly well most times if she was properly flat- tered."[3.14]

Maybe Cook was an ineffective driving instructor, or, more likely, Stein was a difficult student. For whatever reason, there is no end to the stories about her peculiar driving habits. It is often noted, for example, that she could only drive forward, not in reverse. As late as 1933, she still could not back up a car without considerable difficulty. As she writes in her first autobiography (from Toklas' point of view), "She [Gertrude] goes forward admirably, but she does not go backwards successfully. The only violent discussions we have had in connec- tion with her driving a car have been on the subject of backing."[3.15] And Toklas in her own book says that Stein had "a scary habit of talk- ing and forgetting about driving," and that "If the map said Avignon was on the right, and Gertrude preferred the left, she went left."[3.16]

"Gertrude's driving," as recalled by their friend Samuel Steward, "was a wild and won- derful thing. She would see that everyone was in place—Alice usually in front and the guests

■ The only thing she [Gertrude Stein] did, to my knowledge, to which her French friends could have objected morally and maybe legally was to seem often to be about to run them down with her car. Though possessed with lightning-fast reactions and a knowl- edge of how to handle a Ford, she felt she owned the road. She spent a good deal of time driving for visits, on errands, or just for the pleasure of being at the wheel. But she regarded a corner as something to cut, and another car as some- thing to pass, and she could scare the daylights out of all concerned.

—W.G. ROGERS (1948)

■ I happened to be practicing at the piano one day…and suddenly a vacuum cleaner started up just beside the instrument…[As a result] I could imagine what I was doing, but I couldn't actually hear it. But the strange thing was that all of it sounded better than it had without the vacuum cleaner, and those parts which I couldn't actually hear sounded best of all. Well, for years thereafter, and still today, if I am in a great hurry to acquire an imprint of some new score on my mind, I simulate the effect of the vacuum cleaner by placing some totally contrary noises as close to the instrument as I can.

—GLENN GOULD
Glenn Gould Reader
(1984)

and dogs in the back. Then she would climb in, sit down very hard on the rubber cushion, wiggle a few times to adjust herself, clamp her big hands on the steering wheel in a clutch of death, tramp on the starter—and we would be off in a cloud of dust and squawking chickens, roaring at breakneck speed through the quiet country lanes, outraging and terrifying the peasants."[3.17]

Stein even liked to write while sitting in the car. According to Donald Hall, she "sometimes wrote parked in her Ford at a busy intersection in Paris where French law required all drivers to squeeze their klaxons [sound their horns] as they approached cross-streets—because, as she said, the clangor took the top of her mind away."[3.18]

WHILE STEIN may not have owned any of Cook's paintings, she nevertheless admired him so as a person that she wrote at least four short literary pieces (and possibly more) that may have been inspired by him: "What Does Cook Want To Do" (1916), "I Must Try To Write The History of Belmonte" (1916), "Captain William Edwards" (1916) and a screenplay called "A Movie" (1920).[3.19] In addition, she mentions him repeatedly in several of her books, and sometimes at considerable length.

The third paragraph of a brief experimental work titled "I Must Try To Write The History of Belmonte" begins by announcing that "This is going to be the story of Cook." A second later, she returns not to Cook but to a famous

Spanish toreador named Juan Belmonte, whose remarkable feats in the bullring she and Cook had witnessed (while living on Majorca) at a festival in Valencia, Spain. Two paragraphs later, she abruptly changes the subject again: "Cook does and he says and he is kind to all. He has

Figure 3.F
Preparatory pencil sketch by GARY KELLEY of expatriate artists and writers in a Paris sidewalk cafe in the 1920s or 30s.

french as a friend and he speaks Majorcan. He understands all. He is so kind."[3.20] In the remainder of this work, which goes on for a couple of pages, Cook is mentioned twice more specifically by name, but so is Belmonte, and it is never certain whether "he" in the text is referring to one or the other.

At the end of World War I, Stein also wrote what seems to be a screenplay about Cook's and Jeanne's wartime adventures. Titled "A Movie," its unnamed protagonist is an American painter turned taxi driver, who is taught the

■ Cook never talked about his [art]work. Nor did he talk about other people's work. But he was very helpful, a very helpful, kind person.

—CICELY GITTES
(1998)

names of Paris streets by his French mistress, a housekeeper or *femme de ménage* who was born in Brittany. When the U.S. enters World War I, the painter tries to volunteer for the American Army, but the army asks instead that

Figure 3.G and 3.H
At the conclusion of World War I, the Allied armies organized a huge Victory Parade through the streets of Paris on July 14, 1919. In keeping with tradition, it was essential that they pass through the Arc de Triomphe [above, right of center], a monument to the French military and the world's largest victory arch. Passing through the arch on horseback [on facing page] is U.S. Commanding General John J. Pershing.

he continue to pretend to be a Paris taxi driver, while actually working clandestinely for the U.S. Secret Service.[3.21]

In the screenplay, through a series of comical mishaps, this painter and his mistress are credited with capturing two American soldiers who have been embezzling funds from the U.S. Army, and who then, disguised as officers, have fled south on motorcycles. All this comes to light because of an automobile accident that takes place as the painter and his mistress are driving their Renault taxi over the mountains in a snowstorm, in order to visit her relatives in Avignon. He is too drowsy to drive, so she has taken over the wheel when suddenly they collide with the two motorcyclists. The American painter, who sustains minor burn injuries, is rushed to the hospital, but eventually the episode ends with the capture of the two payroll thieves.

Because of this and other exploits, writes Stein (within this screenplay), the American

painter, his Breton mistress, and their little Renault taxi become such celebrities in Paris that, when the war finally ends, they are asked to take part in the famous parade through the Arc de Triomphe, at the request of General Pershing. They and their taxi are placed near the end of that huge procession, just after the armored tanks, with the mistress behind the wheel and the painter in the passenger's seat, waving the American Old Glory in one hand and the French tricolor in the other.

To what extent is Stein's screenplay an account of a genuine, factual event? It is impossible to know because a screenplay, like any work of literary fiction, is free to depart from the facts as it wants. On the other hand, we know from Stein's first autobiography that she

I always remember [Élie] Lascaux the French painter, it was he who having always lived in an isolated country and coming to Paris thought the automobiles going around the Arc de Triomphe were a carousel and it only slowly dawned on him that they were always different cars not the same ones...

—GERTRUDE STEIN
(1973a)

■ Glenway [Wescott, an American writer newly arrived in Paris] impressed us greatly with his English accent. Hemingway explained. He said, when you matriculate of the University of Chicago you write down just what accent you will have and they give it to you when you graduate.

—GERTRUDE STEIN
(1933a)

■ There was also Glenway Wescott but Glenway Wescott at no time interested Gertrude Stein. He has a certain syrup but it does not pour.

—GERTRUDE STEIN
(1933a)

and Toklas really did witness the famous parade through the Arc de Triomphe (from the apartment window of Jessie Whitehead, the daughter of British philosopher Alfred North Whitehead[3.22]). Wrote Stein (speaking as if Toklas): "It was this scene that Gertrude Stein described in the movie she wrote about this time that I [Toklas] have published in *Operas and Plays* in the Plain Edition."[3.23]

Can any of this be verified? At the very least, it would be interesting to find historic film footage of the entire victory parade to determine if it really concludes with a Renault taxi, with an American man (Cook) and a French woman (Jeanne) inside. And did Cook actually work undercover for the U.S. Secret Service? That possibility becomes even more intriguing in view of his later adventures in the Soviet Union.

In 1918, by which time Cook was no longer working as a taxi driver, he again volunteered for the American Expedition Forces, and this time ended up assigned to the 32nd Aero-Engineers Squadron. We know this from various letters he wrote in which he reported to Stein and Toklas that his father had been shipping him a strange assortment of American magazines, while Jeanne had been sending him packages of "roast chicken that never cease to arrive in an advanced state of decomposition."[3.24]

In a letter from the same period, Cook also shared with Stein the news that another artist from Iowa (two years his senior) had written to him at the front. That artist was Sherry Fry, a sculptor from Creston, Iowa, who (like Cook) had studied at the Art Institute of Chicago and in Paris. In 1907, while living in France, Fry had been commissioned to create a sculpture of Mahaska, the 19th-century leader of the Ioway Indians, a statue that still stands today in the town square of Oskaloosa, Iowa. In 1917, Fry had been one of the founders of the American Camouflage Corps, and now he had written to Cook to announce (perhaps as an indirect insult, since Cook was a painter under fifty) that "all the great painters in France under fifty are in camouflage!" **3.25** ■

■ "Bob swore!"—as the Englishman said for "Good night," when he first learnt French, and thought it so like English. "Bob swore," my ducks!

—CHARLES DICKENS
David Copperfield

■ [While visiting New York] the taxis looked different and the trucks completely different. It was like the camouflage in the war. They all meant it to be the same but as it was done by different nations it was not the same. During the war I was interested that the camouflage made by each nation was entirely different from the camouflage made by another nation but I had not expected the cabs and trucks to look different in America from those in France after all there are lots of American cars in France but they did.

—GERTRUDE STEIN
(1973a)

■ Thomas Wolfe says you can't go home again. I say you can—but keep it under an hour and a half.

—LARRY RIVERS
What Did I Do?
(1992)

Four / Purée of Spinach with Croûtons

Returning Home But Not To Roost

COOK AND Jeanne were married at 1:30 in the afternoon on March 2, 1922, with Stein and Toklas standing in as their legal witnesses.[4.1] After years of living together, why would they choose to be legally wed? Cook had just passed forty, while Jeanne was that age or older, so presumably part of the reason was age. They also must have been perturbed (as Stein and Toklas were as well—and would always be) by the absurd necessity, both legal and social, of having to hide their true relationship within the conservative settings of Majorca, or Belgium (where Cook and Jeanne had encountered some kind of banking difficulty, because of their unmarried status), or, in the case of his Iowa relatives, of having to pretend that they did not live together.

In addition, Cook was now employed by the Red Cross, and, given the time frame, their wedding may have been a way to prepare for his departure to a remote relief mission in the Caucasus region of Russia (in the area of Georgia and Armenia), where the people were desperately trying to cope with the combined consequences of the Russian Revolution and a devastating famine. Cook was scheduled to leave for Russia by the end of the month—but

■ I always remember [Pavel Tchelitchew] writing to us the first time he was ever on shipboard and saying how bored he was with the ocean because it was just like the Russian revolution it just kept going up and down and being unpleasant and annoying and upsetting but it never went forward and back it just went up and down.

—GERTRUDE STEIN
(1973a)

———

Figure 4.A
ROY R. BEHRENS
Waistlines Related to Dancing
Visual Poems for Gertrude Stein, 2004.
Digital collage.

was he also still employed by the U.S. Secret Service?

In order to travel to the capital of Georgia (then called Tiflis, now Tbilisi), Cook and his Red Cross associates went by train in a box car, departing from Batoum (now Batumi). Although "something like the army again," it was, said Cook, a "pleasant trip" that took a day and a half, with two nights of continuous travel.[4.2]

"The first night was rather amusing," Cook wrote to Stein, "as we stopped at every station. At first it was a bit exciting as before every stop we were surrounded by a real live howling mob. Of course we were in the dark and keeping quiet, in hopes that our car would not be invaded. There [were] people all over the train on top and on bottom and on all the sides. The crowd[s] however were very nice. When we found out what it was all about we calmed down and went to sleep. It seems that the people had come down from the country to get their seed corn and were taking it back on their backs. Naturally it is to them a matter of life and death and they were all for getting on the train. At every stop our car was opened and when our convoyer explained that we were the American mission they melted as if by magic and stormed another car."[4.3]

WITHIN DAYS of Cook's departure, Gertrude Stein was introduced to the then unknown American artist and photographer Man Ray. Stein, as one author has said, was "as good a

■ William Cook often disappeared and one knew nothing of him and then when for one reason or another you needed him there he was.

—GERTRUDE STEIN
(1933a)

■ Cook was a witness to the first moments of the Russian Revolution. He had unpleasant memories about his stay in that country.

—CRISTOBAL SERRA
(1992a)

sniffer of talent as [Jean] Cocteau," and in her first conversation with Man Ray, she arranged for him to take studio portraits of Jeanne Cook, so that Jeanne could send a (now lost) photograph of herself to her Iowa in-laws, whom she still may not have met.[4.4] This photographic session took place, and, in the end,

Figure 4.B
WILLIAM COOK untitled, no date. Watercolor. Collection of Katherine and Craig Shives.

Man Ray charged 100 francs for a print of Jeanne's portrait.

Cook was stationed in the Caucasus with the Red Cross for nearly two and a half years. Nine months after his arrival, he was joined by his newly-wed wife, who remained with him until June 1924, when they returned to France together.

While living in Russia, the Cooks had tea in Tiflis with the American dancer Isadora Duncan, who was a friend of Gertrude Stein and who, incidentally, as a child, had grown up in the same neighborhood as Stein in Oakland, California. After the Cooks had attended a performance by Duncan at the Tiflis Opera

■ Isadora [Duncan] not only danced but was demanded all over America and Europe. On the Continent she was more widely known than any other American of that decade, including Woodrow Wilson and excepting only Chaplin and Fairbanks, both of whom, via a strip of celulloid, could penetrate to remote hamlets without ever leaving Hollywood. But Isadora went everywhere in the flesh.

—JANET FLANNER
(1972)

■ [Isadora Duncan
was] a woman whose
face looked as if it had
been made of sugar
and someone had
licked it…

—G.B. SHAW
in H. Pearson,
GBS: A Postscript
(1950)

Figure 4.C
WILLIAM COOK
untitled, no date.
Watercolor. Collection of
Katherine and Craig
Shives.

House, Cook sent off a letter to Stein in which he reported that "it was nice to see someone who had come from the land of the free and the home of the brave," but he thought her dancing was "a frost."[4.5] At age forty-five, Duncan was losing her figure, and it was Cook's conclusion that "There is a certain rela-

tion between waistlines and dancing that cannot be gotten away from."

At the same time, Jeanne was increasingly worried about her own waistline. Far more appreciative than Cook of Duncan's performance, she scolded him for his sarcasm, and applauded loudly at the end of Duncan's performance. "She [Duncan] is a compatriot of mine," said Jeanne to Cook. She also reprimanded him for pointing the camera too low when he took snapshots of her, because it showed her waist and hips. "She says one has no need to diet," he wrote to Stein, "if you will hold the camera high enough."[4.6]

It was during their stay in Russia that, at Stein's urging, Cook and Jeanne repeatedly tried to assist the family of Pablo Picasso's wife at the time, the Russian ballerina Olga Khokhlova. Her family was living in Tiflis, and Cook had agreed to pass money to them, which Stein sent to him from Picasso.[4.7]

There is no doubt that by this time Cook and Picasso were acquainted, and at least one Spanish source insists that not only were they friends, they were "great friends."[4.8] That of course is possible, and yet, in 1924, after he and Jeanne had returned to Paris from Russia, he confessed in a letter to Stein that he had difficulty in recognizing Picasso. He wrote: "I think I saw Picasso on the street yesterday, but I am not sure. He was bareheaded and it didn't seem to be his nose and then he was gone, so I will probably never know if it was he."[4.9]

Cook had ambivalent feelings about Russia (as he had about his own homeland). Russia and the U.S., he wrote to Stein and Toklas in 1929, "are the two most interesting countries but me oh my they are so fatiguing to live in."[4.10] On the one hand, he was greatly interested in Russian cultural traditions, and yet, at the same time, he believed that its people were terribly cold (in particular, recalled his Majorcan friend Cristobel Serra, he was "irritated by their inability to understand the 'bourgeois' mentality of Westerners."[4.11])

In addition, he may have been terrified (understandably) by the diabolic roguery of the Soviet secret police (known as the Vecheka or

> ■ America has all that Russia has not. Russia has things America has not. Why will America not reach out a hand to Russia, as I have given my hand?
>
> —ISADORA DUNCAN
> Boston speech (1922)

> ■ During William Morris' last visit to Paris, he spent much of his time in the restaurant of the Eiffel Tower, either eating or writing. When a friend observed that he must be very impressed by the tower to spend so much time there, Morris snorted, "Impressed! I remain here because it's the only place in Paris where I can avoid seeing the damn thing."
>
> —CHARLES KNEVITT
> *Perspectives*
> (1986)

■ The first question anyone asks you on your return from the Soviet Union is: "Were you followed?" Every Western tourist likes to think he was. There is really no fun going to a police state, if you're not followed by someone. In the Hotel Metropole in Moscow I had the feeling I was always being watched, but it was always by other tourists who thought I was *watching them*.

—ART BUCHWALD
More Caviar
(1959)

■ There is a saying in the Soviet Union for the sort of occasion when a sudden silence falls. People do not say "an angel is passing," but "*rodilsya militsionair*"—a policeman has been born.

—ERIK DE MAUNY
Russian Prospect
(1970)

Cheka). Three years after Cook had returned from the Caucasus, he and Stein were driving late at night in a heavy fog on a lonely road near Paris. "Cook had a small open car," Stein remembered (speaking as Toklas), "but a powerful searchlight, strong enough to pierce the fog. Just behind them was another small car that kept an even pace with them, so that when Cook drove faster, they drove faster, and when he slowed down, they slowed down. Gertrude Stein said to him, it is lucky for them that you have such a bright light, their lanterns are poor and they are having the benefit of yours. Yes, said Cook, rather curiously, I have been saying that to myself, but you know after three years of Soviet Russia and the Cheka, even I, as an American, have gotten to feel a little queer, and I have to talk to myself about it, to be sure that the car behind us is not the car of the secret police."[4.12]

COOK'S MOTHER had died suddenly in 1918, while he was serving at the front in the army. Then his father died six years later, while he and Jeanne were in Russia. He was unable to go home for either funeral, but in 1925, he and Jeanne agreed to spend six months in the U.S., partly to acquaint his wife with his relatives and his homeland, and also to participate in the settlement of his parents' estate. They arrived in the U.S. in May 1925 and were back in Europe by early December.

At the top of Cook's list of priorities was his

determination to take Jeanne on a coast to coast sightseeing tour of the U.S. To aid in mapping out the route, one of his brothers sent to Cook in Russia a Rand McNally Auto

Trail Atlas. "It is rather exciting," Cook wrote to Stein and Toklas, "and the number of roads you can take to get places is disconcerting. Jeanne has located Monterrey and wonders if will be as nice as Palma [de Majorca]. I think w will go the northern route and back the south ern. Probably burn up in Arizona but I have always had a feeling that I would not be happy till I had seen Arizona again. I used to like to look out of the car windows it looked so little like Iowa. Practically every town in Iowa has a camp [for automobile tourists] except Independence, and the things that camps will do for you is rather wonderful."[4.13]

Figure 4.D
This is a view of Main Street (looking east) in Independence, Iowa, in the early 30s, nearly coincident with Cook's return to the U.S. for a sightseeing tour.

During their six-month stay in the U.S., they toured the country by automobile from east to west and west to east, visiting such popular tourist locales as Niagara Falls, Yellowstone National Park, Glacier National Park, and the Grand Canyon.

On the return trip from the Southwest, they paused in Iowa for about two months, while Cook worked with his brothers and sister (all of whom had driven home to see the couple) on sorting out their parents' estate. His relatives and the townspeople of Independence were wonderfully kind to Jeanne, Cook reported to Stein, so much so that "she seems to be booked with engagements for the next three weeks." [4.14] He was also able to visit his old friend, Doc McGrady, the physician and farm manager who, years earlier, had encouraged him to paint. McGrady had become blind, yet, despite that handicap, wrote Cook, "he is the best informed man in these parts and I find him just as interesting as he used to be." [4.15]

One day during this visit to Iowa, Cook ran into a nine-year-old boy named James T. Martin, whose family lived on the one of the farms owned by the Cooks, and who would later become an electrical contractor, including work for Frank Lloyd Wright. In the 1990s,

Figure 4.E
WILLIAM COOK
untitled, no date.
Watercolor. Collection of
Katherine and Craig
Shives.

retired and still living in Independence, Martin still recalled the day when he spoke to Cook, who was driving a V8 Cadillac touring car, the largest that Martin had ever seen. "When I expressed so much interest in the car," recalled Martin, "he let me see under the hood and all the other parts of the car, including the box with the tool kits. Then he gave me a ride for several miles. I was very impressed with his kindness. Of course, I knew he was an artist in France and this made a very deep impression on me."**4.16**

About midway through his stay in Independence, Cook ran a wood splinter into the index finger on his right hand, which then became badly infected. Unable to use a typewriter, he sent a handwritten letter to Stein and Toklas, reporting that Jeanne was suffering from terrible homesickness, and suggesting that a letter from them "would cheer her up more than anything else."**4.17**

Leaving Iowa, they drove eastward, deliberately passing through Pennsylvania, with the plan that they would stop for lunch in Allegheny, Stein's birthplace. That did not happen, but they did visit Washington, D.C., and then drove north toward New Haven, Connecticut, where they spent the remainder of their visit with Cook's brother, Robert, at Yale University. ▪

▪ Jeanne Cook had said that in all America there were no lettuces and no salads.

—GERTRUDE STEIN
(1973a)

▪ The internal migrations in America at the same period seem to me fully as important as the transatlantic movement. Many of my own contemporaries… were "escaping" from the Main Streets of their small towns in the provinces to the big cities such as Chicago or New York. They were saying "Good-bye Wisconsin," or good-bye Ohio or Kansas, as they rode eastward to New York…

—MATTHEW JOSEPHSON
(1962)

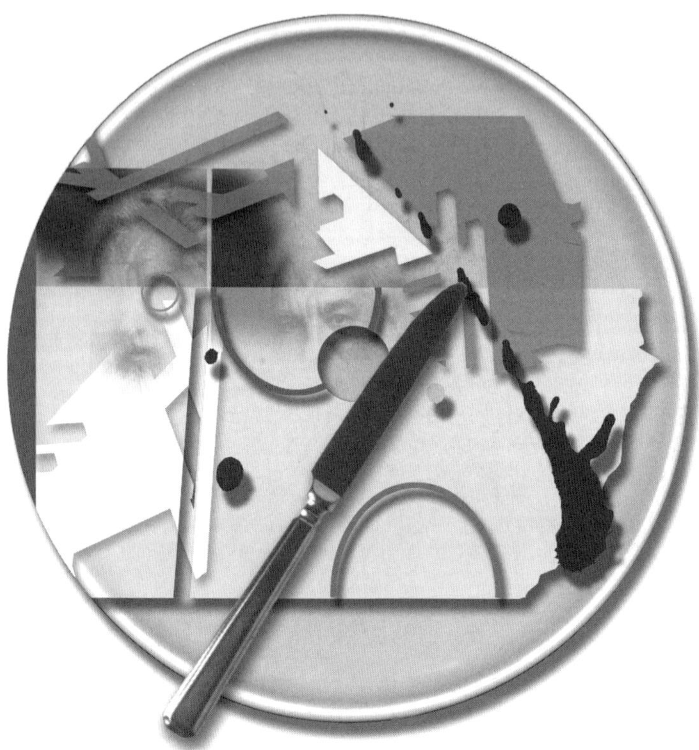

■ In my experience, if you have to keep the lavatory door shut by extending your left leg, it's modern architecture.

—Nancy Banks Smith
The Guardian (1969)

Five / Cheese

The Proprietor of a True Cubic House

SHORTLY AFTER returning to Europe, Cook used part of his inheritance from his parents' estate to purchase a plot of land on which he hoped to build a home in Boulogne-sur-Seine, on the outskirts of Paris. While searching for an architect, he was introduced to the then obscure Le Corbusier by the sculptor Jacques Lipchitz (a friend of Stein), who had just had a similar villa designed by the same architect in the same neighborhood.

Coincident with all of this, although with some hesitation, Le Corbusier had agreed to design a comparable villa for Michael Stein, Gertrude's older brother. He was hesitant to take it on at first because the Steins had furnished their previous home with Italian Renaissance antiques. "Don't buy anything but practical furniture and never decorative furniture," Le Corbusier advised; and, as he explained to Michael Stein, "I have to be very careful when I take [on] my clients so that they don't spoil my house with their furniture."[5.1]

The first formal consultation between the Cooks and Le Corbusier took place on April 28, 1926. They appear to have had very few disagreements during the design process, because the basic plan for the house was completed

■ My assistant, Isadore Grossman, one day came to me in a fury, saying that the teacher had been talking about modern sculpture and a girl had asked him what he thought of the sculpture of Lipchitz. The teacher had had a lump of clay in his hands and had let it fall on the floor, where it splattered, saying that that was a Lipchitz. I only said, "That is a rather interesting idea. I think I might try to make some such sculptures."

—JACQUES LIPCHITZ
(1972)

———

Figure 5.A
ROY R. BEHRENS
Almost Like a Home Tour
Visual Poems for
Gertrude Stein, 2004.
Digital collage.

only three days later on May 1, and the layout was fundamentally the same when construction of the house began in July of that year. In contrast, a number of major revisions were made in the design of the Stein villa, so that construction of that project had still not begun when the Cooks moved into their finished home in March of 1927.[5.2]

On the other hand, not everything went smoothly in the construction of the Cook villa. In early September, for example, Cook was distressed to discover that Le Corbusier (whom he described to Stein in a letter as a "temperamental genius") had mismeasured, so that he mistakenly placed Cook's house outside of the property line, fifty centimeters into his neighbor's yard. "I thought this was a thing that was not according to Hoyle," Cook wrote to Gertrude Stein, "and he [Le Corbusier] told me I seemed to be a type absolutely without gratitude. Gratitude be damned says I—What I want is to have the thing fixed up. Well, it will cost me ten thousand francs before the thing is finished and he is mad because I have no appreciation of the fact that he got me fifty centimeters of land I didn't want."[5.3]

A further complication occurred later, when another misunderstanding arose between architect and client. Le Corbusier may have deliberately underestimated the cost of the project at its outset, in part by allowing for certain details (such as the quality of the window glass) to be determined later. While the architect was on vacation, it was Cook who apparently decided to install regular window glass in the windows on the street façade of the villa, instead of thicker, more costly plate glass.

When Le Corbusier returned, he sent Cook a letter demanding a correction. "I am convinced that you will readily agree to it so as to avoid a serious blemish to your property," the architect wrote, "For you we have made the best of our houses, and one with which we have taken particular trouble. Alas, I fear that you do not appreciate it for what it is, or the distressing incidents which you have caused us would not have happened." After all, he added, "A fine gentleman setting out for a ball would never wear a paper collar with his dinner jacket."**5.4**

Le Corbusier's early buildings are often characterized as the architectural equivalent of cubist paintings, and he himself described Villa Cook as "the true cubic house" (*le vrai maison cubique*).**5.5** The house is literally a cube in the sense that the plan and the elevation are both derived from the same square.

The ground floor of Villa Cook is divided into a car port on one side, and a pedestrian entrance and walkway on the other. Raised above ground by *pilotis* (or stilts) and side wall supports, the actual living quarters are housed in a sculptural two-story box, which begins on the second floor. It has a curiously inverted room arrangement: The bedrooms, dressing room, bathroom, and the original maid's room are all on the second (or lower) level of the

■ When [Jacques] Lipchitz's roof leaked after a rainstorm, wetting the wall beneath and Lipchitz pointed it out to Le Corbusier, his scornful reply was "I'm an architect not a plumber!" Lipchitz accepted his dictum and took his troubles elsewhere.

—Irene Patai
(1961)

■ The house is a machine for living.

—Le Corbusier

house, while the kitchen, dining room, and living room are on the third level. The height of the living room is double, so that it flows up

Figure 5.B
WILLIAM COOK
Self-Portrait, no date.
Intaglio. Current location unknown.

■ "Turbot, Sir,"
said the waiter, placing before me two fishbones, two eyeballs, and a bit of black mackintosh.

—THOMAS EARLE WELBY

into a fourth level, which contains a roof garden and library.[5.6]

Shortly after his clients had moved into their new home, Le Corbusier sent a vase of flowers to Jeanne Cook. In response, Cook sent the architect a note in which he said that "We are more and more pleased with the house day by day. Mrs. Cook was delighted with the superb arrangement of flowers which she received yesterday evening. The living room is full of them, like a field in springtime." Added Jeanne: "We are very happy and grateful that you have managed to produce not only a great house, but a very pretty one, with so much light and sun."**5.7**

While evidently pleased with their new home, the Cooks asked a few years later that it be modified by the addition of a separate maid's quarters in the back, with an outdoor bedroom and recreation area on the floor above. They recommended Le Corbusier to prospective clients, and frequently showed the interior to acquaintances who were planning to build a house.

Over the years, as Le Corbusier became increasingly famous as an architect, the distinction of the Cooks also evolved. As Stein's friend William G. Rogers remarked in his memoir, Cook's distinction soon became not that of an artist but "largely as the occupant of a house built by Le Corbusier."**5.8**

A few years later, when Cook and Jeanne were visited at Villa Cook by W.R. Kellogg, a friend of Mrs. A.D. Grant (who had been Cook's third grade teacher in Iowa), Kellogg described the meeting to her in a letter. William Cook, wrote Kellogg, "is a very agreeable and polished man of the world and has a real artist's home which he had built on his own occupancy, after original and unique plans. There is a roof garden and the rooms have many specimens of paintings both by himself and his wife, who speaks little English."**5.9**

ALTHOUGH THE specific circumstances are unclear, at some point in his forties or fifties, it

■ Manhattan is a great unfilleted sole spread out on a rock.

—LE CORBUSIER

■ [When asked to name his favorite animal] Filet of sole.

—SALVADOR DALI

■ Karl Marx suffered from the same kind of illusions as poor Le Corbusier, whose recent death filled me with immense joy. Both of them were architects.

—SALVADOR DALI
Conversations with Dali

■ Once in Spain a society for the protection of animals was founded which was hard up for money. They put on some large bullfights.

—KURT TUCHOLSKY

■ I remember that Cook was always very nice about Le Corbusier, and I have an idea that Le Corbusier was rather a stinker.

—CICELY GITTES
(1998)

appears that Cook was troubled by severe self-doubt and depression. Not surprisingly, given the lackluster progress of his artist's career, he had finally reached the conclusion that he would never be a successful painter, much less an important one. By one account, in the years that followed the death of his father, he destroyed all his own artworks in his possession, completely gave up painting, and decided that, from then on, his life would be given to reading and traveling.**5.10**

While there is no reason to question this, the time of its occurrence is confusing, because his father died in 1924, yet as late as four years later, Cook was still painting Cézanne-inspired landscapes, and in fact he was busily finishing work for a public exhibition.

We know that Cook was painting in 1928 because that is the year he shipped a landscape painting to Mrs. Grant, his former grade school teacher (mentioned earlier), along with a couple of letters. They had last seen each other in 1925, when, by coincidence, both he and she had been in his hometown (of Independence, Iowa) at the same time. He told her then that his early instruction from her had been instrumental to his development, and, as a gesture of his appreciation, he wanted to send her a painting from France.

That painting was shipped from Paris to Jamestown, North Dakota (where Mrs. Grant had moved after her retirement), in October 1928. Inside was a letter that read: "The landscape here is painted at Bandol in the Var [in the south of France]. The white road in the foreground is the road going to Toulon, the French naval base, about twelve miles away. It is a beautiful country and so highly cultivated that the hills about seem to be worked like a tapestry. The country is old and mellow, and the

Figure 5.C
WILLIAM COOK
Bandol Landscape, 1928.
Oil painting. Collection
of Bill Klotzbach.

roots of the grape vine in the foreground— whisper it not in our prohibition country— have probably been guilty of producing more than one bottle of mellow wine."**5.11**

Soon after, unsettled parts of his parents' estate made it necessary for Cook to return alone to the U.S. in early 1929, only months in advance of the stock market crash that would trigger the Depression. He wrote to Stein and Toklas from New York on March 19 that "Conservative people say the stock market must crash by fall. May be who knows."**5.12**

While staying with his brother in New

■ [Being from England] I didn't know anything about America. I thought to myself, if Cook is the average American, then the Americans must be very clean, very pleasant to sit with.

—CICELY GITTES
(1998)

■ If you are lucky enough to have lived in Paris as a young man, then wherever you go for the rest of your life, it stays with you, for Paris is a moveable feast.

ERNEST HEMINGWAY
Letter (1950)

Figure 5.D
Cover of the Vintage Books edition of Gertrude Stein's *The Autobiography of Alice B. Toklas.*

Haven, he prepared to leave for another return to his Iowa hometown. But a terrible blizzard suddenly dumped 42 inches of snow on the Midwest, and when he was finally able to get there, he was so overwhelmed by estate-related matters that he lost track of his European correspondence. "Yes," he wrote to Gertrude Stein, "I got your letter in New Haven or rather Iowa, and I thought I answered it but the pigs and the thoroughbred cows and bulls and calves and everything were taking up so much time maybe I didn't."[5.13]

MEANWHILE, IN France in 1929, Stein and Toklas decided to rent a summer home in Bilignin, near the town of Belley, where they had lived in a hotel during previous summers. As it turned out, this was a crucial decision because, a few summers later, in 1932, it was at Bilignin that Stein was able to produce her most popular book, *The Autobiography of Alice B. Toklas,* in a brief period of only six weeks.

Some critics think this book by Stein is her most important achievement, while others contend the opposite. It is surely her most widely read book, her least enigmatic (although it has no lack of puzzles), and it was also her first commercial success. It was published in the U.S. by Harcourt Brace, serialized in advance of publication in the *Atlantic Monthly,* and offered by the Literary Guild as a book club choice. The first printing of 5,400 copies was sold out nine days before the book came out. At the end of its first year, from the American edition alone, she had earned what today is equivalent to about $85,000. French and Italian translations came out in 1934 and 1938, respectively.

The *Autobiography* was not only a financial success, it was also widely praised by influential literary critics. It was acclaimed by William Troy in *The Nation* as "one of the richest, wittiest and most irreverent [literary memoirs] ever written,"[5.14] while Cyril Connolly maintained that it was "a model of its kind."[5.15] At the same time, because of the scandalous things Stein had said about so many of her famous acquaintances, it prompted a flood of rebuttals, and resulted in various people (Braque, Matisse, and Ernest Hemingway, among others) refusing to speak to her.[5.16]

But even when reactions were unfavorable, Stein was being talked about, and her book sales were thereby increasing. "All my congratulations on your success," Cook wrote to her, "It seems the whole world is as interested in you as if you had kidnapped the President, and it may be that the world is interested in the right things after all."[5.17]

To which Stein replied: "Everything has been said about the book but you have said more. Alice and I were both awfully moved by your letter. It touched us both right there. I am awfully happy you feel as you do about it, it means a lot to me…[You yourself should] write a book, and tell all the things I did not remember."[5.18]

In an undated reply, Cook admitted that he had already "been working quite hard for a

[Jeanne Cook] was a very natural person…She was like so many peasant women, who are around and they do what they're supposed to do. They usually wash floors and do that kind of thing…And she was that sort. And Cook liked it. He liked her very simple. She could read and write of course, but she was a very simple French woman. She used to say funny things sometimes, and he always remembered them, to just make one laugh.

—CICELY GITTES
(1998)

■ During the most austere phase of Analytical Cubism, when he and Braque were working in closely related styles, Picasso one day went to look at his friend's latest work. Suddenly, he became aware that there was a squirrel in the picture, and pointed it out to Braque, who was rather abashed at this discovery. The next day Braque showed him the picture again, after reworking it to get rid of the squirrel, but Picasso insisted that he still saw it, and it took another reworking to banish the animal for good.

—H.W. JANSON
"Chance Images" in
Dictionary of the History of Ideas
(1973)

year on a book, but it's about Iowa. Don't worry, I have a bit of sense…I'm not writing a book about what you forgot. Not that. It's about other things and maybe it will get done or maybe not."**5.19**

Somewhat later, perhaps in 1934, Cook sent another letter to Stein in which he mentioned that he was still working on a memoir of growing up in Iowa. At that point, he and Jeanne were residing at Villa Cook, and his work was interrupted by a visit from William G. Rogers (Stein's friend, mentioned earlier), who had come to be given a tour of their house. "When he rang the bell," Cook wrote to Stein, "I was writing about a youth of twelve going to the World's Fair in 1893, the train just coming in to Chicago early in the morning. The first thing he remembers seeing in Chicago was a dead horse lying dead in one of the streets in the outskirts. He was white and a nice horse like one of [Felix] Potin's [delivery horses]. He thought he wouldn't like Chicago. He never did."**5.20**

In view of the earnings from *The Autobiography of Alice B. Toklas*, Gertrude Stein's literary agent had been trying to persuade her to write a sequel, as scandalous and accessible as the first. She was also being urged to return to the U.S. for a book publicity tour. But Stein was almost sixty years old, and had always been susceptible to anxiety. She had not set foot in her homeland for thirty years, and the mere prospect of traveling so far and speaking to so many strange (and potentially hostile) audiences was enough to terrify her. For a long time she declined, and then, in July of 1934, she began to warm up to the idea. She wrote to Carl Van Vechten (her close friend and, later, her literary executor, who was a journalist turned novelist from Cedar Rapids, Iowa), "I am slowly but steadily getting pleased about getting over there and so is Alice, we begin to talk about it quite now as if we were going and even beginning to feel confident about it."[5.21]

That same month, Cook wrote to Stein and Toklas to say, "We will follow your trip to America with the greatest interest. Am very glad you are going. There is nothing to be nervous about. You will have a wonderful time and the thing to do is to go."[5.22]

Soon after, Stein replied to him that "Yes we are going over there and the Time Club [sic] of the town of the University of Iowa [in Iowa City] invites us [to speak]…Is that anywhere near Independence [Iowa, Cook's hometown]? We would love to lecture in Independence but I am afraid it is too far away. It almost feels to us like a home tour."[5.23]

AS IT happened, Stein and Toklas arrived at New York harbor on October 24, 1934, and returned to Paris on May 4, 1935. During a stay of about six months, they had, as Cook predicted, a marvelous time, traveling by airplane and automobile across the entire U.S., giving lectures at schools and museums. Stein lectured in the East at the Museum of Modern Art, Columbia University, Princeton University, Bryn Mawr College, Harvard University, and

I liked the [news] photographers, there is one who came in and said he was sent to do a layout of me… [consisting of] four or five pictures of you doing anything. All right I said what do you want me to do. Why he said there is your airplane bag suppose you unpack it, oh I said Miss Toklas always does that oh no I could not do that, well he said there is the telephone suppose you telephone well I said yes but I never do Miss Toklas always does that, well he said what can you do, well I said I can put my hat on and take my hat off and I put my coat on and I can take it off and I like water I can drink a glass of water all right he said do that so I did that and he photographed while I did that and the next morning there was the layout and I had done that.

—GERTRUDE STEIN
(1973a)

■ Paris: Wet pavements. And lights—everywhere there are lights! I come upon a man at an outdoor café. It is André Malraux. Oddly, he thinks that I am André Malraux. I explain that he is Malraux and I am just a student. He is relieved to hear this, as he is fond of Mme. Malraux and would hate to think she is my wife. We talk of serious things, and he tells me that man is free to choose his own fate and that not until he realizes that death is part of life can he really understand existence. Then he offers to sell me a rabbit's foot. Years later, we meet at a dinner, and again he insists that I am Malraux. This time I go along with it and get to eat his fruit cocktail.

—WOODY ALLEN
Side Effects
(1981)

Radcliffe College (her alma mater). In the Midwest, she was featured at the University Chicago, and in Wisconsin, Minnesota, Michigan, Indiana, and Ohio. On the West Coast, she spoke in Pasadena, Oakland, Berkeley and San Francisco. And in the South, she lectured at Richmond, Charlottesville, Charleston, Atlanta, New Orleans, and St. Louis. All this took place in addition to any number of other speeches, newspaper and radio interviews, public appearances, private parties, and reunions with friends she had formerly known.[5.24]

Unfortunately, because of unavoidable circumstances, she was never able to visit Iowa. On a winter flight from St. Paul, Minnesota, to Chicago, where she was scheduled to connect with a chartered flight to Iowa City, bad weather forced her plane to land in Waukesha, Wisconsin, a suburb just west of Milwaukee. At the very least, she had hoped that her plane might fly over Cook's hometown of Independence, during daylight hours, so she could see it from the air. But a major blizzard had hit Chicago, and instead they had to take a train from Milwaukee to Chicago, and to cancel her engagements in Iowa City. Had she been able to get there, she had been scheduled to lecture at The Times Club or (as it was sometimes called) The Society for the Prevention of Cruelty to Speakers,[5.25] the gatherings of which were held in downtown Iowa City, on the second floor of what is now the Prairie Lights Bookstore. There is today a sign on the wall of the bookstore's coffee shop, marking the site where, had it not been for a snow-storm, Gertrude Stein *would have* spoken there.

Writing to Cook from New York, Stein expressed her disappointment at not being able to see Iowa: "We almost saw your birthplace Cook but the airplane struck a blizzard and would not fly and so we didn't, but it is a nice country all the same."[5.26] To which he replied, "Too bad the plane wouldn't take you over Independence in a blizzard. It used to be lovely in a blizzard. I don't know now.

"They are nice out there. You will like them if you get out there.

"We see they have found you a club.

"They should. You must be having a wonder-ful time, some day you will tell us about it."[5.27]

And of course Stein did exactly that. She told the entire world all about "what happened after *The Autobiography of Alice B. Toklas*" and about her adventures in America in a second autobiography (just as she had been advised by her literary agent) titled *Everybody's Autobio-graphy*, published in 1937. ■

Figure 5.E
Cover of the 1973 Vintage Books edition of Stein's *Everybody's Autobiography*, with a photograph of a famous sculpture of her (looking very Buddha-like) by American artist Jo Davidson.

■ Of course I liked Charlie Chaplin [whom she met in Hollywood] he is a gentle person like any Spanish gypsy bullfighter he is very like my favorite one Gallo who could not kill a bull but he could make him move better than any one ever could and he himself not having any grace in person could move one as no one else ever did, and Charlie Chaplin was like Gallo.

—GERTRUDE STEIN
(1973a)

■ Picasso, you and I are the greatest painters of our time, you in the Egyptian style, I in the modern.

—Henri Rousseau
(Man Ray 1979)

Six / Berries and Fruit

Almost Thou Persuadest Me
To Be A Picassoite

WHILE LIVING in Russia, Cook had written to Stein that Jeanne and he had often talked about "passing our old age in the Balearics."[6.1] Perhaps in anticipation of that, as early as 1929 they had begun to return to Majorca for part of the year. By then it had become well known as an exotic, affordable haven for expatriate artists and writers.

Among the writers living there were the British poet Robert Graves, his mistress Laura Riding, and American novelist Robert McAlmon, who later said of William Cook that he was "an unassuming American painter who was content to be known as 'a farmer from Ohio.'" In their first encounter, McAlmon was surprised to find that Cook knew all about his work, including McAlmon's novel about the American Midwest, titled *Village*, in which Cook's favorite character was Daisy the cow. He admired, he said, the "cowiness of the cow."[6.2]

Perhaps also with a view toward retirement, the Cooks moved out of Villa Cook in the mid-1930s. They leased it and then moved to Rome, thinking they might settle there. But Mussolini and the Fascists had taken over Italy, and it soon became apparent that most of Cook's old artistic friends (among them Giorgio de

gertrude steinie
let down her heinie
all on a summer's day
as it fell out
they all fell in
the rest they ran away

—E.E. CUMMINGS
Selected Letters
(1969)

—

Figure 6.A
ROY R. BEHRENS
Life Is Short, Art Is Long
Visual Poems for
Gertrude Stein, 2004.
Digital collage.

■ And then I saw Picasso, and he said no, never get the same kind of a dog again never, he said I tried it once and it was awful, the new one reminded me of the old one and the more he looked like him the worse it was. Why said he, supposing I were to die, you would go out on the street and sooner or later you would meet a Pablo, but it would not be I and it would be the same. No never get the same kind of a dog, get an Afghan hound, he has one, and Jean Hugo had said I could have one, but they are so sad, I said, that's all right for a Spaniard, but I don't like dogs to be sad, well he said get what you like but not the same, and as I went out he repeated not the same no not the same.

—GERTRUDE STEIN
(1940)

Chirico) had moved elsewhere. What were the alternatives? "Have told Jeanne that if she prefers we can go and live in Iowa," Cook wrote to Stein and Toklas, but "she seems to have leanings toward Palma [de Majorca], as I have myself." He went on: "She says she likes Iowa, but has the feeling that Paddy [their dog] would not be happy there…"**6.3**

Unfortunately, when at last they did decide to move to Majorca, they were met by immediate hazards. The Spanish Civil War had begun in July of 1936, and right-wing insurrectionists (led by Francisco Franco, among others) had launched an effort to overthrow the existing government, which was headed by the left-wing Popular Front. Located strategically off the coast, the Balearic Islands were eventually targeted by the rebels. As a result, the Cooks, along with about a hundred other Americans, were forced to leave Majorca, and were taken by boat to Marseille, France. Prior to that evacuation, the city had been bombed daily for ten days, and then placed under martial law. In a letter to Stein and Toklas, Cook recalled the details of an especially harrowing morning:

"Jeanne was at the central market [in Palma] one morning, things being rather scarce in Terreno and the bombardment being always at eleven, she went down early and got caught in the market where three bombs fell. She came running in to Juan's, our coffee man, the one who used to keep the road house in Cas Catala, just as a woman had been blown up in front of his door. He was jittery and would not sell her [Jeanne] coffee. He didn't know where she had gone. As I was to meet her there I got a bit nervous but found her in one of the big cellars under the market drinking a good bottle of wine with a wonderful collection of Majorcan women and telling them it was nothing and they should wait till the Big Bertha [a devastating World War I long-distance German cannon] got to working on them before getting excited."**6.4**

After the evacuation to Marseille, the Cooks decided to move elsewhere, in part because, as Cook told Stein, "France is beyond our means." By winter, they were back in Rome, where they were more amused than frightened by their first public sighting of El Duce (Mussolini), of whom it is typically noted that, despite his detestable methods, he made the trains run on time. "The parade of Roman Eagles gave me quite a kick," Cook wrote in a letter, "Rome is a lovely place to live, and it's so clean, so orderly, you wouldn't know it from the times before the big war."**6.5**

Meanwhile, Cook's siblings had been sending him travel money, in the hope that Jeanne and he would choose to escape the turmoil in Europe, and return to Iowa to live. But they continued to live in Rome, and in late February of 1937, in anticipation of their fifteenth wedding anniversary, Cook wrote to their marital witnesses that "the only thing we will be able to do will be to drink [to] your health on this day...So, at one-thirty, next Tuesday, consider yourselves being drunk to."**6.6**

One of the nice things about Rome is that one never knows exactly what time it is. No two clocks ever agree. One perceives the moment through a soft focus, in which the edges of all duties and commitments are happily cushioned.

—RUDOLF ARNHEIM
Parables of Sun Light
(1989)

He used to be the *roi de pipi* and then there was none.

—GERTRUDE STEIN
in a letter to
Carl Van Vechten about the
kidney problems of her
chihuahua, Pépé

■ Gertrude Stein. She lies half stretched out on her black horsehair sofa, her hand buried in her poodle's white wool. She looks calm and strong as a mono-lith; she might be ten centuries old, that is, she has the youth and serenity of a mountain. She tells me that one day she opened a book of mine and saw that my sentences were really sentences; she adds that she read only one sentence!

—JULIAN GREEN
(1964)

At the same time, he reported with pride that Villa Cook had been featured in a new book on Le Corbusier's work, on view at book-stores at the time. Three years earlier, the house had been rented to tenants who, accord-ing to their old neighbor Jacques Lipchitz, "have done the house over…and seem to have done it very well."[6.7] (A few years later, when Cook and Jeanne were visiting Paris and dropped by to see their famous home, they were surprised by its garish interior trimmings: "Our house is velvet carpeted and lace curtained and oil heated and everything. I guess we were very pleased but it looked very different from when we left it."[6.8])

Less than two months after that wedding anniversary, a small village in the Basque region of northern Spain was destroyed by a massive bombing attack. More than 2,500 townspeople were killed or wounded in a raid that was carried out clandestinely by Nazi warplanes, at the behest of the Fascist insurgents. Later that year, at the Spanish Pavillion at the Paris Exposition Universelle, Picasso (a native Spaniard, still living in Paris) exhibited what is now widely regarded as his second most important painting, titled *Guernica*, in which he expressed his rage at the merciless slaughter of his civilian countrymen.

There may or may not have been a link between this high visibility protest by Picasso and the subsequent publication of a new book by Gertrude Stein, simply titled *Picasso*. When it was first published in 1938, Cook sent Stein a letter to say how much he enjoyed it, that he was "delighted, charmed and fascinated."[6.9] At the same time, in a lengthy afterthought, he also made it clear that he believed that Picasso's celebrity was as much the result of Stein's promotion of him as it was of Picasso's accomplishments as an artist. Her book on Picasso, wrote Cook, "runs along with a swing in which there isn't a hitch, it jumps and bounds at times and beyond a doubt you have done the Picasso legend and it will stay that way.

"It's as it should be, for I have always maintained that you made Picasso; without you he would have melted off somewhere, into something else, you have kept him and made him Picasso, so, now it is only right that you should have made Picassoism, and you have.

"You have made Picassoism in the same sense that St. Paul made Christianity.

"Now, I can say with King Agrippa, Gertrude, almost thou persuadest me to be a Picassoite; and say it in all seriousness. Even if not quite, you won't care; there will be enough you will persuade completely, and look at all those you have before the book; for as I have always said, you made him. And he is not a mean thing to have made, nor is the book."[6.10]

COOK VISITED his native land for the last time in August of 1939, only weeks in advance of the Nazi invasion of Poland and the subsequent start of World War II. He and Jeanne had been visiting in Paris, and he sailed from France to the U.S. on a ship called *Manhattan*, in part

Figure 6.B
Cover of the 1973 Vintage Books edition of Gertrude Stein's *Lectures in America*.

Figure 6.C
WILLIAM COOK
untitled, 1948.
Oil on board. Collection
of Celia and George
McHenry.

▮ [Gertrude Stein
referred to Boston
publisher Edmund
Brown as Honest-
to-God-Brown] in
imitation of William
Cook's phrase when
everything was going
particularly wrong.

—GERTRUDE STEIN
(1933a)

in order to attend the New York World's Fair.
In a letter to Stein and Toklas, he voiced his
concern about the capriciousness of the Third
Reich. "Jeanne is staying on in Paris," he wrote,
"where she thinks it will be cooler, which it
doubtless will unless Hitler has a brainstorm."

6.11 Cook returned to Paris on
September 30, three days after the
surrender of Warsaw.

Meanwhile, the U.S. government
had decided to recognize the new
Spanish leadership of Franco. The
bombing of Majorca had ceased,
and American citizens were once
again allowed on the island. In
October 1939, Cook and Jeanne
returned at last to Palma, this time
to make it their permanent home.

In the same year, Gertrude Stein, who was of
Jewish heritage, was warned by the American
consulate that France was likely to be invaded
by the Nazis, and that she would be wise to
leave. But instead, she and Toklas moved out to
their Bilignin summer home and later to a
nearby town called Culoz. In June of 1940, Paris
was overtaken by the Germans.

At the end of January of 1941, Cook wrote
to Stein from Majorca to say that he had
recently learned that Villa Cook had been
damaged, but not irreparably, by the fighting. In
a subsequent letter, he also told them that
Jeanne and he were making plans to spend
their wedding anniversary at a bullfight.**6.12**

Paris was liberated by the American Army in

August of 1944. A few months later, Stein and
Toklas returned home to Paris, and soon after
wrote to Cook and Jeanne. Cook replied that
he was "delighted to have your postcard this
morning and know Paris is still standing. Heard
from the [Villa Cook] house agent and the
storage people that everything seems to be all
right. We had heard nothing of the house since
we heard it had been pretty well shattered in
the first bombardment of Paris, and were naturally quite worried."[6.13]

Within days of the French liberation, partly
through the efforts of CBS war correspondent
Eric Severeid, Stein had broadcast a victory
radio speech to the American public. "What a
day is today that is what a day it was day before
yesterday, what a day!" her talk began, "I can
tell everybody that none of you know what this
native land business is until you have been cut
off from that same native land for years. This
native land business gets you all right. Day
before yesterday was a wonderful day."[6.14]

By this time, she had also written a third volume of autobiography, titled *Wars I Have Seen*.
Published in 1945, it sold more than 10,000
copies, with the result that she and Toklas
become as much a Paris tourist attraction as
the Eiffel Tower or the Cathedral of Notre-
Dame. Flocks of American soldiers showed up
at their apartment at 35 rue Christine, in the
St. Germain section of Paris, where they had
moved in 1938. "It is extraordinary," she said to
Cecil Beaton, "the way these boys come to see
us. They come to see Pablo [Picasso] and they

I reached Paris
towards the end of
May. The chestnut
trees were in flower in
the boulevards, the
tulips gleamed in the
Luxembourg Gardens
and wherever one
looked one saw young
men and girls kissing
and holding hands.
Everything spoke of
love and I felt lost and
sad because I had no
one. Then suddenly I
did have someone. As I
was buying a shirt in
the Magazin du Louvre
an English girl asked
what was the French
for button. Bouton, I
replied, we both
laughed and I asked
her to lunch. By the
time dessert was
served we were kissing
like everyone else.

—GERALD BRENAN
Personal Record
(1975)

It is very serious. They [the American soldiers with whom she had talked] have lost faith. They are devitalized. All you Americans are devitalized, you have lost that something that drove the pioneers onwards, the founders of the United States. What's the reason for this? All Americans are job-minded, they think of nothing but their job. A job is the answer to all their problems. The soldiers go home with the fixed idea of finding a job. That is what is weakening the whole nation.

—GERTRUDE STEIN
(Green 1964)

come to see me. They don't go to anybody else and I don't believe they come to see us because we're celebrities, but because we're rebels. They know Pablo and I have had to put up a fight in our time and we've won."**6.15**

Soon after she began to write patriotic articles for American magazines, and to tour U.S. Army bases in Europe, as ways to openly show her support for the liberation of Europe. It was during one of these tours, in December 1945, while she was speaking to GIs in Belgium, that she began to experience intestinal pains of such severity that she could no longer ignore them. Yet, she continued to refuse surgery for the next six months, until she had become so ill that in mid-July of 1946, she had to be taken by ambulance to an American hospital in Neuilly, France. There, it was discovered that she had an advanced case of intestinal cancer.

On July 22, just five days before she died during surgery, Stein received advance copies of her newly published book, titled *Brewsie and Willie*, a memoir of her experiences with American soldiers in Europe. Among its pages, there is the following passage: "…I just tell you and though I don't sound like it I've got plenty of sense, there aint any answer, there aint going to be any answer, there never has been any answer, that's the answer."**6.16**

Later, her companion Alice B. Toklas, in her own autobiography, recalled how Stein had returned to those same thoughts in the last hours of her life: "I sat next to her," Toklas recalled, "and she said to me early in the afternoon, What is the answer? I was silent. In that case, she said, what is the question? Then the whole afternoon was troubled, confused and very uncertain, and later in the afternoon they took her away on a wheeled stretcher to the operating room and I never saw her again."[6.17]

WILLIAM COOK was sixty-five when Gertrude Stein died. Living on Majorca at such a great distance, it appears that he was not aware that she had been ill for months. In fact, only a few weeks before her death, he sent her a letter (without any mention of her illness) in which he asked if she could phone the real estate agent for Villa Cook, who had failed to keep him up to date on the condition of the house.

Figure 6.D
JEANNE MAOLLIC COOK untitled, no date. Oil painting. Collection of Katherine and Craig Shives.

In the same letter, he talked nostalgically about Majorca, describing how it differed from the days of their first visit in 1913. "Every one here paints or writes or both and bullfighting," he told her, "One of our friends who did the drawings for the bullfight Sunday does all three. The island is becoming so talented it is pitiful." And among the Majorcan artists was Jeanne. She "paints every day," Cook reported, "and gets on quite well at the exhibitions."[6.18]

His tone is fatigued and sardonic; he was presumably still depressed. He makes no mention of the fact that he too has been actively painting again. An American artist named Archie Gittes, who had also gone to

Figure 6.E
ARCHIE GITTES
Es Malalt [self-portrait],
1943. Photograph
courtesy of the Gittes
family. The painting is on
loan by them to the
Circulo de Bellas Artes,
Palma de Majorca.

school at the Art Institute of Chicago (in the 1920s), and whom Cook may have met through Stein, had slowly been coaxing him out of his artistic lethargy.

The Gittes family (Archie and his British-born composer wife, Cicely) had settled in Majorca in the 1930s, perhaps as early as 1932, and had at first resided in Deyá, a small fishing village, where their next door neighbor was the British poet Robert Graves. One of Archie Gittes' finest paintings is a portrait of Graves, now in the collection of the Museum of Majorca.[6.19]

Over the years, the Gittes and the Cooks became active participants in the Majorcan artistic community, along with a cluster of painters, sculptors and art critics (nearly all of Spanish heritage), among them Miguel Angel Colomar, Mario Verdaguer, Juan Antonio Fuster Valiente, Violeta Dreschfield, Antonio Sabater, Ramon Nadal, Pedro Sureda, Jaime Juan, Luis Derqui, Gabriel Fuster Mayans, and Jean Bonet.

Whenever they went to Majorca, Cook and Jeanne invariably stayed in Terreno, albeit at different specific locales, on Calles Dos de Mayo, Calvo Sotelo, and Son Catleret. According to Cristobal Serra, Cook "lived" on the island in the fullest sense of the word. "He was as Majorcan as anyone," wrote Serra in a posthumous tribute to Cook, "but, more than that, he was a pro-active Majorcan, in the sense that he wanted to widen the doors and the windows of culture. Majorcan art is far more indebted to him than most people realize, because even though he was not avant-garde and had few disciples or followers, he understood art with a fullness and a balance that prompted the island to slowly become more tolerant of new artistic tendencies. You could say that it was Cook who brought badly needed oxygen to the local atmosphere."[6.20]

In this same essay, Serra also spoke of what it was like to encounter Cook on the street in Palma de Majorca in his later years. It was at once obvious that he was an American, wrote Serra, because his attitude was a blend of both "cheerfulness and candor." He had certain daily habits, so that it was common to "see him crossing El Borne, in the direction of the Figaro Café, which is no longer standing, where he would invariably order an espresso. He always carried a large basket, in which he would transport packages, vegetables, books and flowers. These flowers, which he used as decorative arrangements in his home, were also the subjects he painted sometimes," while the books he carried with him "were almost always new, recently published books, which he liked to share with his friends and to comment on at social gatherings. Cook was a voracious reader. He admired Henry Miller, who was one of his friends in Paris."[6.21]

Figure 6.F
ARCHIE GITTES
Cicely Foster, 1937.
Terra cotta sculpture, with actual necklace. Photograph courtesy of the Gittes family. Location of original artwork unknown.

ARCHIE AND Cicely Gittes left Majorca in 1948 to settle permanently in the U.S. But Cook and Jeanne continued to live on the island of Majorca. Cook died eleven years later in 1959, and Jeanne died two years after that.

As he aged, Cook's strength had diminished. "His last years," Serra concluded, "were saddened and embittered by a serious illness that slowly undermined his health…"[6.22]

William Edwards Cook died at his home in Terreno on November 10, 1959 at age 78. He

and his beloved Jeanne were buried in a small religious cemetery in Genova, a district of Palma de Majorca, where today their vault-like tombs remain.

Nine years earlier, when the Cooks had returned to Paris for a brief visit, they had seen Alice B. Toklas, who was 73 that year. He wrote a letter to his Iowa relatives in which he reported that "Alice Toklas is still going strong—although she looks about a hundred but I suppose we do too."[6.23]

As it turned out, although she was older than Cook by four years, Alice outlived everyone else in the story (even Le Corbusier), dying in 1967, just a few months short of age 90.

But surviving all the participants in this historic tragicomedy is the architectural setting, the house called Villa Cook that stands at 6 rue Denfert Rochereau in Boulogne-sur-Seine. In recent years, it was described in an architects' manual as "almost in original state" and "slightly worn."[6.24] The building's reputation has not just survived, it has burgeoned: While never regarded as a major work by Le Corbusier, it is a Modernist landmark that is of increasingly importance because it was the first implementation of what he and Pierre Jeanneret, his cousin and partner, defined as the "Five Points of a New Architecture." ■

Figure 6.G
Recent photograph of the wall of above-ground vaults where William and Jeanne Cook are buried, in a religious cemetery in Genova, on the outskirts of Palma de Majorca. Photograph courtesy of Jeff Flood (1998).

■ When Gertrude Stein was a young girl, the twentieth century was approaching like a distant train whose hoot you could only just hear. A whole age was about to end. Nations would rededicate themselves, an entire generation bite into a fresh loaf, turn over a new leaf...tremble, pray. Despite this threat from the realm of number, though, most of the world went on as before, repeating itself over and over in every place, beginning and rebeginning, again and again and again.

—WILLIAM H. GASS
(1978)

What is sauce for the goose may be sauce for the gander, but it is not necessarily sauce for the chicken, the duck, the turkey or the guinea hen.

—ALICE B. TOKLAS
(1954)

Seven / Liqueurs

The Past Is Not Gone
Nor Is Gertrude

◼ Gertrude Stein. She mentally turns over a considerable number of peculiar ideas and displays them forcefully, one hand in the pocket of an ample embroidered waistcoat of the kind worn by 18th-century financiers, the other twisting and smoothing her cropped gray hair. Her eyes are large and beautiful, there is something brave and open in her expression…Her voice is deep and manly; when she laughs, she laughs in bursts that show every tooth in her head.

—Julian Green
(1964)

◼ He [Henri Matisse] used his distorted drawing as a dissonance is used in music or as vinegar or lemons are used in cooking or egg shells in coffee to clarify.

—Gertrude Stein
(1933a)

◼ I have just come from France drinking pastis with the mayors of villages in the Basses-Alpes, but it was really work as I had to lecture and speak, too, and I am very hoarse because it is difficult talking French with false teeth when you are not used to it.

—T.S. Eliot
Letter to Djuna Barnes
(1948)

◼ He: Tell me, dear, how did you find the caviar?
She: Oh, quite by accident, when I lifted the quail egg.

—Anon
French cartoon caption

◼ I like a view but I like to sit with my back turned to it.

—Gertrude Stein
(1933a)

—

Figure 7.A
Roy R. Behrens
*What Is Sauce
for the Goose*
Visual Poems for
Gertrude Stein, 2004.
Digital collage.

■ Propaganda is not French, it is not civilized to want other people to believe what you believe because the essence of being civilized is to possess yourself as you are, and if you possess yourself as you are you of course cannot possess any one else, it is not your business. It is because of this element of civilization that Paris has always been the home of all foreign artists, they are friendly, the French, they surround you with a civilized atmosphere and they leave you inside of you completely to yourself.

—Gertrude Stein
(1940)

■ One of our best family treats was Grandma Page's stone soup, and I never thought there was anything odd about it.

The family was visiting in Bloomington and cash was tight all around, so Grandma would clean up a big stone and cook it with water and lots of grass, especially grass that came with seeds. I'd help and so did everybody else. We chopped up some carrots and onions and Grandma added a little Tabasco sauce.

She simmered this mix slowly, eventually bringing it briefly to a boil. It made a tasty soup.

—Dan Rather
I Remember
(1991)

■ It is said that the way to cook a *galah* [a pink-breasted cockatoo, in the Australian outback] is to put the bird and a rock into a pot and bring it to a boil. Continue cooking. When the rock is soft enough to eat, throw away the galah and eat the rock.

—Anon
Australian folklore

■ Dawn comes slowly but dusk is rapid.

—Alice B. Toklas

■ The past is not gone—nor is Gertrude.

—Alice B. Toklas

■ But of all the footmen the lowest
class is literary footmen.

—WILLIAM HAZLITT
Sketches and Essays
(1839)

Footnotes

BEFORE TURNING to specific matters, it may be helpful to make note of the following: The titles and order of the book's chapters are taken from an exotic French dinner menu, reported by Alice B. Toklas (1954) on page 13 of her own famous cookbook. All English-language biographical notes on William Cook indicate that he was born in Independence, Iowa, in 1881, yet several Spanish sources state that he was born in Des Moines, Iowa, sometimes in 1879. From Iowa archives (newspaper clippings and legal documents), it seems certain that the Cooks were never residents of Des Moines, and that he was born not in 1879 but in 1881. In studies of Gertrude Stein or Le Corbusier, Cook is sometimes listed as "an American journalist," but, as far as I can determine, he was always a visual artist, never a journalist. Whatever Cook's virtues, one of his persistent faults was a failure to put a date of completion on his artwork or to reliably date the letters he wrote. In 1992, for example, when an exhibition of his paintings was held posthumously at the Centre Cultural de la Misericordia in Palma de Majorca, only five of 80 paintings had dates on them. Likewise, a considerable portion of the corrrespondence between the Cooks (William and Jeanne) and Stein and Alice B. Toklas is also undated, although a date can be surmised in some cases from the postmark, or from knowledge of events discussed. In the following footnotes, unless otherwise noted, the Cook and Stein letters cited are in the Collection of American Literature in the Beinecke Library at Yale University. —RRB

Two: Mirrored Eggs

2.1 Stein said this about Oakland, California, not (as is often mistakenly claimed) Allegheny, Pennsylvania, or "some Midwestern town." **2.2** The 118-acre Père-Lachaise cemetery, the former farm of Father Lachaise (confessor to Louis XIV), contains the gravesites of scores of historic celebrities, including Stein and Toklas. The former would have loved the misspelling of Allegheny as she found endless delight in the inability of French officials to spell that and Pennsylvania. **2.3** It was Minnesota-born writer Robert McAlmon who said that Cook described himself as an Ohio farmer (Smoller (1975)). He may have been mistaken, or possibly Cook did indeed say that, as a quiet way of poking fun at Eastern city dwellers who are so rarely able to distinguish between Iowa, Ohio and Idaho. **2.4** While Fadiman's phrase is memorable, whatever Stein was, at least in art historical terms, she was *not* the mother of Dada. **2.5** Stein (1968), p. 70. When writing to Stein, Cook signed all his letters "Cook," but writing home, he signed them "Will." **2.6** Cook letter dated July 23, 1938. **2.7** Stein (1973a), p. 224. **2.8** For more on the halcyon days of Independence, Iowa, see Petersen (1965) and Hall (1965). **2.9** The Gedney hotel and opera house was destroyed by fire in March 1945. I first wrote about this in 1963 as a high school student, at which time, not knowing why Williams had chosen the name, I wrote to the Gedney pickle company in Chicago and asked if they were somehow affiliated with Williams (who had contacts in Chicago). They were not. **2.10** Williams named the 300-acre area in honor of Rush Lake, an Iowa-born tax collector from Kansas City; he also later named his sons Rush and Park. The racetrack's location had formerly been the Buchanan County fairgrounds. Williams' house is still standing, but, as this book was being prepared, despite community protests, the large Queen Anne-style horse barn was demolished by a bulldozer, to make way for a fastfood drive-in and gas station. **2.11** Stein (1973a), p. 224. **2.12** In "What Does Cook Want to Do," Stein (1955) describes Cook's parents as having "a daughter and three sons," but his father's obituary and other sources indicate that there were three additional sons. Two of them, Justin Jr. (Eddie) and Nelson (Nell), died during childhood, at 4 and 2 respectively. Another son, named Horace, was impaired by scarlet fever as a child, then died of influenza at age 35 in 1919. This is based on information found by R.H. Behrens. **2.13** Stein letter to Cook (c1933, n.d.). **2.14** Stein (1955), pp. 31-32. **2.15** Regarding Tabor, see Behrens (2000). **2.16** See Serra (1992b) and Cook (n.d.), both of whom imply (although one may be based on the other) that Cook met Sargent when he was still a high school student, which sounds far-fetched. When interviewed, Cicely Gittes (1998)), who knew Cook in Paris and Majorca, agreed that the adult Cook was acquainted with Sargent, but perhaps not as early as high school. **2.17** For information on Cook's Chicago exhibition record, see Falk (1990). **2.18** The Sherman mansion, located at 1501 Woodland Avenue, has housed the Des Moines Women's Club since 1907. **2.19** Stein (1933a), p. 152. **2.20** National Academy of Design records indicate that Cook enrolled in life drawing class on October 4, 1902, and remained there during that academic year. **2.21** The source for the Renoir and Bouguereau story is P. and L. Murray, *A Dictionary of Art and Artists* (Penguin Books, 1976), p. 64. **2.22** Serra (1992b). **2.23** MacKenzie (1907). **2.24** Ibid. **2.25** According to Richardson (1996), it was André Salmon who titled the painting, while Picasso denied that there was any link to Barcelona. **2.26** This famous remark by Braque has withstood all sorts of translations. Richardson (1996) suggests that he only intended to compare Picasso's achievement to the daring exploits of performing fire-eaters. **2.27** Richardson (1991), p. 475. **2.28** Serra (1992a). **2.29** Ibid. **2.30** Toklas (1963). **2.31** Ibid. **2.32** Ibid., p. 28.

Three: Cold Ham with Lettuce Salad

3.1 Stein (1933a), p. 152. **3.2** Cook letter (c1913, n.d.). **3.3** Ibid. **3.4** Cook letter (1913, n.d.). **3.5** Gittes (1998). **3.6** Stein (1933a), p. 176. **3.7** Cook letter (c1914, n.d.). **3.8** Stein (1933a), p. 199. **3.9** Toklas (1963), pp. 87-88. **3.10** Gittes (1998). **3.11** Cook letter (August 4, 1924). Regarding Stein's lack of interest in Cook's activities as an artist, his Majorcan friend Cristobal Serra said (when visited in Palma de Majorca by Rosalind Moad in May 1992) that, as of 1915-16, Cook "had not painted anything to interest Gertrude Stein" (Moad 1995). **3.12** Cook letter (January 12, 1916; mailed together with an earlier unsent letter dated December 25, 1915). **3.13** Stein (1933a), p. 206. **3.14** Ibid. **3.15** Ibid. **3.16** Souhami (1992), p. 131. **3.17** Steward (1977), p. 11. **3.18** D. Hall, *Life Work* (Boston: Beacon Press, 1993), pp. 58-59. **3.19** Stein scholar Rosalind Moad argues persuasively in her doctoral dissertation (Moad 1995), that Stein may have used Cook and Jeanne Maollic as subjects of a number of short written pieces, some of which were never finished. While the four most often cited are "What Does Cook Want To Do" (1916), "I Must Try To Write The History of Belmonte" (1916), "Captain William Edwards" (1916), and "A Movie" (1920), she also suggests that a second screenplay, titled "Jeanne la Bretonne" (c1915), and two other obscure (and, I believe, as yet unpublished) texts, titled "Mrs. Edwards" (1913) (at that time in Majorca, notes Moad, Jeanne was listing herself as Mrs. Edwards Cook) and "In the Grass (On Spain)" (1913), may have sprung from Stein's attempts to make word portraits of the Cooks. **3.20** Stein (1968), p. 70. **3.21** Ibid., pp. 395-397. **3.22** Mellow (1975), p. 297. **3.23** Stein (1933a), pp. 191-192. **3.24** Cook letter to Stein and Toklas, reprinted in Gallup (1953), p. 127. **3.25** For more on Fry, Stein, Picasso and camouflage, see Behrens (2002).

Four: Purée of Spinach with Croûtons

4.1 The Cook marriage is referred to in several of his letters to Stein and Toklas (making note of the anniversary), for example, one on March 4, 1923, and another on March 3, 1937. **4.2** Cook letter dated April 1, 1922, reprinted in Gallup (1953), pp. 145-146. **4.3** Ibid. **4.4** For details, see Foresta (1988), p. 109. In my contacts with Cook's surviving relatives, I have not been able to find Man Ray's photograph(s) of Jeanne, and indeed, so far I have not found a single photograph of either Jeanne or

William Cook (there are no photographs of him or Jeanne in this book). [4.5] Cook letter dated October 7, 1923. [4.6] Ibid. [4.7] Cook letters dated June 21 and August 8, 1923. [4.8] Cook and Picasso are described as being great friends in Cook (n.d.). [4.9] Cook letter dated August 23, 1924. [4.10] Cook letter dated September 25, 1929. [4.11] Serra (1992a). [4.12] Stein (1933a), p. 291. [4.13] Cook letter dated February 10, 1925. [4.14] Cook letter dated September 14, 1925. [4.15] Ibid. [4.16] Letter to the author from James T. Martin, Sr., dated July 20, 1996. [4.17] Cook letter dated October 26, 1925.

Five: Cheese

[5.1] Patai (1961), pp. 228-229. [5.2] See Benton (1987). [5.3] Cook letter dated September 8, 1926. [5.4] Benton (1987), pp. 158-159. [5.5] Gans (1987), p. 53. [5.6] A lengthy account of Villa Cook, with plan and elevation diagrams, and various photographs of both the exterior and interior, can be found in Benton (1987). [5.7] William and Jeanne Cook letter to Le Corbusier dated March 9, 1927, as quoted in Benton (1987), p. 161. [5.8] Rogers (1948), p. 115. [5.9] Kellogg letter to Mrs. A.D. Grant dated May 7, 1930, in the collection of Bill Klotzbach. [5.10] Cook is described as having destroyed all his paintings, following his father's death, in Cook (1992). [5.11] Cook letter to Mrs. A.D. Grant dated October 24, 1928. This is one of three letters from Cook to Mrs. Grant, in the collection of Bill Klotzbach. [5.12] Cook letter dated March 19, 1929. [5.13] Cook letter dated September 25, 1929. [5.14] From review in *The Nation*, September 6, 1933. [5.15] See C. Connolly, *Previous Convictions* (NY: Harper and Row, 1963). [5.16] For an account of the resulting controversy, see Souhami (1991), Chapter 12. [5.17] Cook Letter dated October 1, 1933. [5.18] Stein letter to Cook (c1933, n.d.). [5.19] Cook letter (c1934, n.d.). [5.20] Cook letter (c1934, n.d.). [5.21] Stein letter to Carl Van Vechten, as quoted in Souhami (1991), p. 201. [5.22] Cook letter (c1934, n.d.). [5.23] Stein letter to Cook (c1934, n.d.). [5.24] For an account of Stein's book promotion tour, see Stein (1973a). [5.25] See Mellow (1975), pp. 474-475. For those who would like to more about the Times Club in Iowa City, a highly amusing account can be found in Petersen (1962). [5.26] Stein postcard to Cook dated January 7, 1935. [5.27] Cook letter dated June 21, 1935.

Six: Berries and Fruit

[6.1] Cook letter dated March 4, 1923. [6.2] McAlmon's satirical novel about a small midwestern town was published in 1924, but he and Cook apparently met for the first time in 1932, at which time both were living on Majorca, as described by Smoller (1974), p. 250. Perhaps Stein sent a copy of *Village to Cook* when it first came out, and when Cook replied, she forwarded his letter to McAlmon who then (according to Ford (1975), pp. 55-56) copied the following portion into his scrapbook: "*Village* amused me tremendously [wrote Cook]. I was especially taken by Daisy the cow. Am quite familiar with cowology and she is the most cowy cow in literature. The fact that she was outraged in her higher cow nature will go a long way to keep her place and her memory green and it will be long before another cow will replace Daisy. It seems to me that she really marks the entry of cows into literature, anyway she far surpasses anything that could have been done. The whole book is interesting, and mainly wonderfully done." [6.3] Cook letter dated July 12, 1934. [6.4] Cook letter dated August 7, 1936. [6.5] Cook letter dated November 2, 1936. [6.6] Cook letter dated February 24, 1937. [6.7] Cook letter dated November 16, 1934. [6.8] Cook letter dated June 8, 1938. [6.9] Cook letter dated March 27, 1938. [6.10] Ibid. [6.11] Cook letter dated August 8, 1939. [6.12] Cook letters dated January 30 and February 25, 1941. [6.13] Cook postcard dated March 14, 1945. [6.14] Stein quoted in Simon (1994), p. 188. [6.15] See Beaton (1961). [6.16] Stein (1946). [6.17] Toklas (1963), p. 173. [6.18] Cook letter dated May 15, 1946. [6.19] See Gittes (1987) and (1991). [6.20] Serra (1992b). [6.21] Ibid. [6.22] Ibid. [6.23] Cook letter to Helen Cook (wife of his brother, Roy Cook) dated July 9, 1950, in the collection of Douglas and Ruth Hamilton. [6.24] Gans (1987), p. 53. ∎

Gratuities
Acknowledgements

SURELY MY least favorite part of producing a book is the acknowledgements section. Not because I don't enjoy thanking people (that in itself is pleasurable), but because I have such dread of inadvertently omitting someone. One solution is to not thank anyone by name, in which case all ones friends can feel equally slighted. That said, let me offer some background:

I've been researching the friendship between William Cook and Gertrude Stein for about 14 years. One regret I have is that I didn't finish this book a few years earlier, so that I could have presented it to an old friend, an Iowa attorney and district court judge named William G. Klotzbach, who died while this project was still in process. As a high school student, I was Bill's janitor; I was the kid who swept the steps of his old second-story law office (using that oily red sweeping compound) on Main Street in Independence, Iowa. He was also the first person to buy one of my paintings, while I was still in high school. More recently, when I moved back to Iowa in 1990 and began to unearth Cook's remains (figuratively speaking), it was Bill (who was a leading contributor to the town's historical society) who excitedly offered assistance, in part because one of his relatives was Mrs. A.D. Grant, Cook's third grade teacher, to whom that grateful artist shipped a French landscape painting in 1928. That painting had passed down to Bill and for years it had been hanging in his and Mary's living room, only steps from that (godawful) painting of mine. It was Bill who then alerted me to the identities and whereabouts of Cook's relatives, nearly all of whom, as it turned out, have Cook's paintings in their homes, along with a handful of letters and some news clippings.

During this research marathon, one of the highlights was an exhibition of 14 paintings by William and Jeanne Cook (borrowed mostly from his Iowa relatives), which I curated. Titled "The Man Who Taught Gertrude Stein to Drive: Paintings by William E. Cook," it was held at the Gallery of Art at the University of Northern Iowa from February 19 through March 13, 1996. It was a greatly rewarding event, in part because so many of Cook's relatives came to the opening from various parts of the Midwest. That exhibition came about through the efforts of Dr. William Lew (then Head of the UNI Department of Art) and Matthew DeLay (Director of the Gallery of Art), and was encouraged by various faculty grants from the UNI Graduate College and the Dean of the College of Humanities and Fine Arts.

At about the same time, I was fortunate to meet one of the country's leading authorities on Gertrude Stein, when Bruce Kellner (author of *Carl Van Vechten and the Irreverent Decades* and *A Gertrude Stein Companion*) was invited to Cedar Rapids, Iowa, to lecture on Van Vechten. It was Bruce who read an early draft of this book. He also put me in contact with another Stein scholar, Ulla Dydo (author of *A Gertrude Stein Reader* and *Gertrude Stein: A Language That Rises*), who in turn referred me to one of her former doctoral students, British scholar Rosalind Moad. The latter had recently visited Palma de Majorca, was very much aware of Cook, and had written her dissertation on the literary projects that Stein had begun while vacationing there. It was also Rosalind who lent me her copy of the full-color catalog of a major Cook exhibit that had taken place in Palma de Majorca in 1992, and who so kindly shared with me relevant aspects of her research. I am grateful for the insight and assistance from these three scholars, but I also want to make it clear that they are not responsible for my research errors.

Through Rosalind, I also learned about 750 pages of correspondence between Cook and Stein at the Beinecke Library at Yale University, photocopies of which I was able to buy. That huge rich resource, which I supplemented by internet searches and by perusing the memoirs of other Modern-era expatriates, led slowly to other discoveries. I was especially lucky to find Cicely (née Foster) Gittes, a 95-year-old British-born composer, and the widow of American painter Archie Gittes, who had been closely acquainted with William and Jeanne Cook in Paris as well as Majorca. Through the kind assistance of her son, Anthony Gittes, I was able to arrange for a tape-recorded interview with Cicely Gittes (which was actually conducted by her granddaughter, Stephanie Gittes), in which she shared her memories of the Cooks, Stein, Toklas, Picasso, Robert Graves, Juan Miro and others. Using the internet, I also made contact with Jeff Flood, an American residing in Palma de Majorca, who was wonderfully helpful in finding the Majorcan burial sites of William and Jeanne Cook.

In addition, all sorts of other people helped: Librarians, archivists, translators (Jaime Gomez and frje echeverria), townspeople, my graphic design colleagues (Phil Fass, Aaris Sherin, Gary Kelley and Mike Wilson), my former teachers, Cook's relatives, the Gittes family, my own relatives (my mother, who first introduced me to books and encouraged my interest in drawing; my brother, who, under different circumstances, might well have been an historian; and my older sisters, who have always encouraged my efforts), my remarkable students (during 33 years of eventful teaching), and a long list of loyal and tolerant friends who—by this time—would probably not care to hear any more about this tiresome hobbyhorse.

As listed in the bibliography, parts of this book were published before (in different form) in articles in *Tractor: Iowa Arts and Culture* (1998) and *Iowa Source* (1999). The plate-like illustrations that begin each chapter are my own digital collages, while other illustrations are vintage images (many from the Library of Congress) in the public domain, or, as cited in the caption that accompanies each illustration, are used here by permission from family members, or from private or public collections. In preparing this book, an extensive effort was made to identify copyright holders of illustrations and to obtain their permission. If brought to the attention of the publisher, any credits that are listed incorrectly or were omitted inadvertently will gladly be corrected in subsequent printings.—RRB ■

Bibliography
Works Consulted and Cited

Agree, W. and B. Rose (1984). *Patrick Henry Bruce: American Modernist*. NY: Museum of Modern Art.

Allen, T. (1977). *Americans in Paris*. Chicago: Contemporary Books.

Allen, W. (1978). "Twenties Memory" in *Getting Even*. NY: Vintage Books.

Archer-Straw, P. (2000). *Negrophilia: Avant-Grade Paris and Black Culture in the 1920s*. NY: Thames and Hudson.

Beaton, C. (1961), *The Wandering Years: Diaries: 1922-1939*. Boston: Little, Brown.

Behrens, R.R. (1998). "Cook, His Wife, Two Thieves and the Pope" in *Tractor: Iowa Arts and Culture*. Vol 6 No 1 (Winter), pp. 31-33.

_______ (1999). "Le Corbusier's Iowa Client" in *Iowa Source*. Vol 32 No 1 (February), p. 9.

_______ (2000). "Four Seasons on an Iowa Farm: The Paintings of Robert Tabor" in *Iowa Heritage Illustrated*, (Spring), pp. 36-48.

_______ (2002). *False Colors: Art, Design and Modern Camouflage*. Dysart, Iowa: Bobolink Books.

_______ (2002). *The Man Who Taught Gertrude Stein to Drive: Cook, Stein and Le Corbusier* [booklet]. Dysart, Iowa: Bobolink Books.

Benton, T. (1987). *The Villas of Le Corbusier*. New Haven: Yale University Press.

Bridgman, R. (1970). *Gertrude Stein in Pieces*. NY: Oxford University Press.

Brinnin, J.M. (1959). *The Third Rose*. Boston: Little, Brown.

Burns, E., ed. (1973). *Staying on Alone: Letters of Alice B. Toklas*. NY: Liveright.

______ ed. (1986). *The Letters of Gertrude Stein and Carl Van Vechten*. NY: Columbia University Press.

Carpenter, H. (1988). *Geniuses Together: American Writers in Paris in the 1920s*. Boston: Houghton Mifflin.

Cook, W.E. (n.d.) Entry for "William E. Cook (1879[sic]-1959" in *Las Baleares y Sus Pintores (1836-1936)*. Luis Ripoli / Paradelo.

Cook, W.E. (1992). "Biographical Notes" in *William E. Cook* [exhibition catalog]. Palma de Majorca: Centre Cultural de la Misericordia, Sala Guillem Mesquida.

Crunden, R. M. (1993). *American Salons: Encounters with European Modernism 1885-1917*. NY: Oxford University Press.

Curtis, W.J.R. (1986). *Le Corbusier: Ideas and Forms*. NY: Rizzoli.

Duryea, N.L. (1927). *Mallorca the Magnificent*. NY: Century.

Dydo, U., ed. (1993). *A Gertrude Stein Reader*. Chicago: Northwestern University Press.

______ (2003) *Gertrude Stein: A Language That Rises*. Chicago: Northwestern University Press.

Falk, P.H., ed. (1990). *The Annual Exhibition Record of the Art Institute of Chicago 1888-1950*. Sound View.

Flanner, J. (1972). *Paris Was Yesterday*. London: Angus and Robertson.

Ford, H. (1975). *Published in Paris: American and British Writers, Printers, and Publishers in Paris, 1920-1939*. NY: Macmillan.

Foresta, M., et al. (1988). *Perpetual Motif: The Art of Man Ray*. NY: Abbeville Press.

Franck, D. (2001). *Bohemian Paris: Picasso, Modigliani, Matisse, and the Birth of Modern Art*. NY: Grove Press.

Gallup, D., ed. (1953). *The Flowers of Friendship: Letters Written to Gertrude Stein*. NY: Alfred A. Knopf.

Gans, D. (1987). *The Le Corbusier Guide*. NY: Princeton Architectural Press.

Gass, W. H. (1970). "Gertrude Stein: Her Escape from Protective Language" in *Fiction and the Figures of Life*. NY: Alfred A. Knopf.

______ (1978). "Gertrude Stein and the Geography of the Sentence" in *The World Within the Word*. NY: Alfred A. Knopf.

Gittes, A. (1987). *Archie Gittes: Exposicio Antologica* [exhibition catalog]. Palma: Museu de Mallorca, Conselleria d'Educacio i Cultura.

______ (1991). "Acclaimed Artist Archie Gittes, 88" [obituary] in *Melrose Free Press*, Melrose, Massachusetts (August 29).

Gittes, C. (1998). Tape-recorded interview of Cicely Foster Gittes.

Glassco, J. (1970). *Memoirs of Montparnasse*. Toronto: Oxford University Press.

Gosling, N. (1978). *The Adventurous World of Paris 1900-1914*. NY: William Morrow.

Graves, R. (1965). *Majorca Observed*. Garden City: Doubleday.

Green, J. (1939). *Personal Record 1928-1939*. NY: Harper and Brothers.

______ (1964). *Julian Green: Diary 1928-1957*. K. Wolff, ed. NY: Harcourt, Brace and World.

Hall, R., ed. (1965). *Golden Years of Independence: Special Centennial Edition of the Bulletin-Journal, 1865-1965*. Vol 100 No 43 (October 22). Independence, Iowa: Bulletin-Journal and Conservative.

Josephson, M. (1962). *Life Among the Surrealists*. NY: Holt, Rinehart and Winston.

Kellner, B. (1968). *Carl Van Vechten and the Irreverent Decades*. Norman: University of Oklahoma Press.

______ ed. (1987). *Letters of Carl Van Vechten*. New Haven: Yale University Press.

______ ed. (1988). *A Gertrude Stein Companion: Content with the Example*. NY: Greenwood Press.

Kluver, B. and J. Martin (1994). *Kiki's Paris: Artists and Lovers 1900-1930*. NY: Harry N. Abrams.

Lipchitz, J. (1972). *My Life in Sculpture*. NY: Viking.

Loeb, H. (1959). *The Way It Was*. NY: Criterion.

McAlmon, R. and K. Boyle (1968). *Being Geniuses Together*. NY: Doubleday.

Mackenzie, R. (c1907). "Portrait of the Pope" in *Chicago Daily News* [issue date about June 14].

Man Ray (1979). *Self-Portrait*. NY: McGraw-Hill.

Mellow, J. R. (1975). *Charmed Circle: Gertrude Stein and Company*. NY: Avon.

Moad, R. (1995). *1914-16: Years of Innovation in Gertrude Stein's Writing* [dissertation]. England: University of York.

Mott, F.L. (1962). "The Society for the Prevention of Cruelty to Speakers" in *The Palimpsest* (March). Iowa City: State Historical Society of Iowa.

Patai, I. (1961). *Encounters: The Life of Jacques Lipchitz*. NY: Funk and Wagnalls.

Paul, E. (1942). *The Last Time I Saw Paris*. NY: Random House.

Petersen, W. J. (1965). *The Lexington of the North* in *The Palimpsest* (special issue). Vol XLVI No 10 (October). Iowa City: State Historical Society of Iowa.

Putnam, S. (1947). *Paris Was Our Mistress: Memoirs of a Lost and Found Generation*. NY: Viking.

Richardson, J. (1991). *A Life of Picasso. The Early Years: 1881-1906*. NY: Random House.

Richardson, J. (1996). *A Life of Picasso. Volume II: 1907-1917*. NY: Random House.

Rogers, W. G. (1948). *When This You See Remember Me: Gertrude Stein In Person*. NY: Rinehart.

Root, W. (1987). *The Paris Edition: The Autobiography of Waverley Root*. San Francisco: North Point Press.

Rorem, N. (1966). *The Paris Diary of Ned Rorem*. NY: Braziller.

Sabartés, J. (1949). *Picasso: An Intimate Portrait*. London: W.H. Allen.

Serra, C. (1992a). "William Cook and His Friends" in *William E. Cook* [exhibition catalog]. Palma de Majorca: Centre Cultural de la Misericordia, Sala Guillem Mesquida.

______ (1992b). "William E. Cook Obituary" in *William E. Cook* [exhibition catalog]. Palma de Majorca: Centre Cultural de la Misericordia, Sala Guillem Mesquida.

Shattuck, R. (1968). *The Banquet Years*. NY: Random House.

Simon, L. (1977). *The Biography of Alice B. Toklas*. NY: Doubleday.

______ (1994). *Gertrude Stein Remembered*. Lincoln: University of Nebraska Press.

Smoller, S. (1975). *Adrift Among Geniuses*. University Park: Pennsylvania University Press.

Souhami, D. (1992). *Gertrude and Alice*. San Francisco: Pandora/Harper Collins.

Stein, G. (1920). *Operas and Plays*. Paris: Plain Edition.

______ (1933a). *The Autobiography of Alice B. Toklas*. New York: Harcourt Brace.

______ (1933b). *Matisse Picasso and Gertrude Stein*. Paris: Plain Edition.

______ (1940). *Paris France*. London: B.T. Batsford.

______ (1955). *Painted Lace and Other Pieces*. New Haven: Yale University Press.

______ (1962). *Selected Writings of Gertrude Stein*. Edited by Carl Van Vechten. New York: Random House.

______ (1968), *Geography and Plays*. NY: Something Else Press.

______ (1973a). *Everybody's Autobiography*. NY: Vintage Books.

______ (1973b). *Lectures in America*. NY: Vintage Books.

Stendhal, R., ed. (1994). *Gertrude Stein in Words and Pictures*. Chapel Hill: Algonquin Books of Chapel Hill.

Steward, S. M. (1977). *Dear Sammy: Letters From Gertrude Stein and Alice B. Toklas*. Boston: Houghton Mifflin.

______ (1984). *Parisian Lives*. NY: St Martin's Press.

Thomas, E.F., ed. (1942). *The Paris We Remember*. NY: D. Appleton-Century.

Toklas, A. B. (1954). *The Alice B. Toklas Cook Book*. NY: Harper and Brothers.

______ (1958). *Aromas and Flavors of Past and Present: A Book of Exquisite Cookery*. NY: Harper and Brothers.

______ (1963). *What Is Remembered*. NY: Holt, Rinehart and Winston.

Turner, E.H., et al. (1996). *Americans in Paris (1921-1931)*. Washington DC: Counterpoint.

Weiss, A. (1995). *Paris Was a Woman: Portraits from the Left Bank*. San Francisco: Harper San Francisco.

Wineapple, B. (1996). *Sister Brother: Gertrude and Leo Stein*. NY: Putnam. ∎

Literature / Art / Architecture
Biography / Women's Studies

ISBN 0-9713244-1-7
$17.95

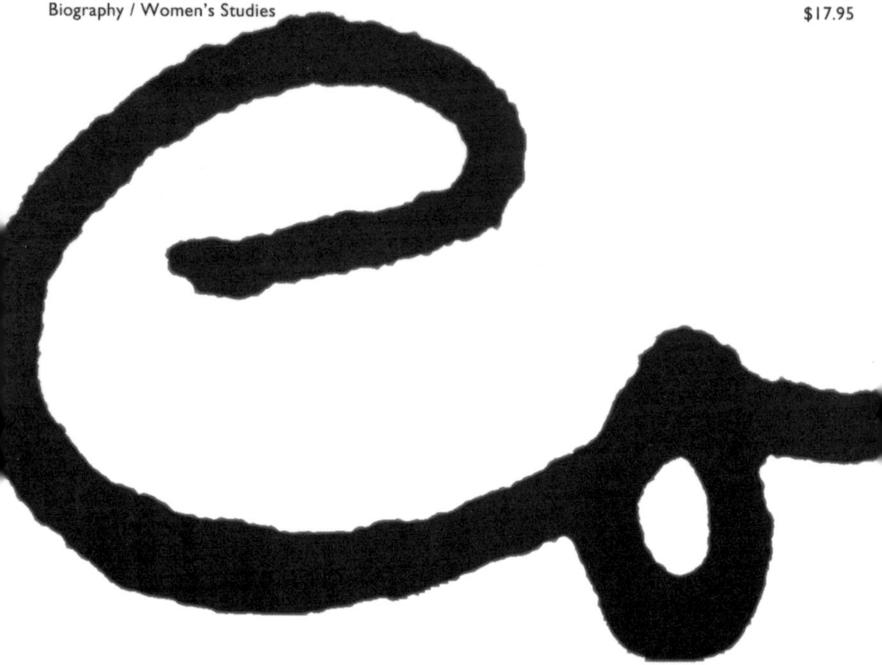

Copies of this book can be ordered directly from Bobolink Books, 2022 X Avenue, Dysart, Iowa 52224-9767 USA. Send check or money order (no credit cards) for $17.95 per copy. Add $2.00 postage and handling for first book by USPS Media Mail, plus $1.00 for each additional copy. Add appropriate sales tax if Iowa resident. If questions, send an e-mail to <ballast@netins.net>. Copies are also available by special order through any major bookstore, or online at Amazon.com (search for title and author, then click link to *new and used*).